Uoniam quidē
multi conati sū
ordinare narra
tionem que innobis ⁊
pletæ sunt rerum si
cut tradiderunt nobis
qui ab initio ipsi uidē
runt ⁊ ministri fuerū
sermonis uisum ē ⁊ mihi
adsecuto principio omni
bus diligenter excondine
tibi scribere obtime
theofile ut cognos
cas ueritum ∴

THE

PICTS

AND THE

SCOTS

THE
PICTS
AND THE
SCOTS

*Lloyd and
Jenny Laing*

A Sutton Publishing Book

This edition published in 1998 by Wrens Park Publishing, an imprint of
W.J. Williams & Son Ltd

This book was designed and produced by
Alan Sutton Publishing Limited, an imprint of Sutton Publishing Limited
Phoenix Mill · Thrupp · Stroud · Gloucestershire GL5 2BU

A catalogue record for this book is available from the British Library

ISBN 0 905 778 227

*Jacket illustration: Hilton of Cadboll Stone (© The Trustees of the National Museums of Scotland);
Frontispiece: The reverse of the Aberlemno churchyard cross (RCAHMS)*

Typeset in 10/12pt Bembo.
Typesetting and origination by
Sutton Publishing Limited.
Printed in Great Britain by
WBC Limited, Bridgend, Mid-Glamorgan.

Contents

We would like to thank James Kenworthy of Nottingham University for reading the entire manuscript to its great advantage.

Introduction

The Picts and the Scots are best known for one reason: their stormy relationship in the fourth to eighth centuries AD which led to the eventual establishment of modern Scotland. Roman historical sources relate that the Picts came from the North and raided Roman Britain in the last days before the Anglo-Saxon conquest of England. The Scots, possibly taking advantage of the removal of Roman troops from Britain early in the fifth century, arrived in western Scotland from Ireland to establish their hold on the area. Thus far the story is easy to follow, yet the Picts and Scots have left a tangle of myths, archaeological facts and historical snippets which have perplexed scholars.

Firstly, who were they? If this question had been asked even thirty years ago, it would have been answered almost exclusively in historical terms. A little was known archaeologically from the investigations at Dunadd in Argyll, one of the strongholds of the Dark Age Scots, and quite a lot was known about the sculptures set up by both Picts and Scots in various parts of their territories. But no overall archaeological picture could have been built up of their world, and no assessment made of the way in which it reflected the world of their contemporaries, or differed from it. The picture is still tantalizingly inadequate, but thanks to research carried out in recent years it is at least possible to attempt the survey that this book represents.

The word 'Pict' is a Roman one and was used from the late third century AD onwards to describe people living north of the Forth–Clyde line. The term, perhaps one of abuse, meant 'the painted people', and was probably an allusion to the designs with which they were said to tattoo their bodies. Whether it was confined to a particular group of northern people, or much more loosely to anyone who lived beyond what had been the Antonine Wall, is not clear, but it seems most likely that it was employed very imprecisely to mean anyone in northern Scotland who was a threat to Roman Britain. This fact alone has caused some obscure reasoning, for it might be expected that such disparate groups would not leave clear and definitive remains in the archaeological record. When we come to look at the finds and settlements it is possible to isolate some which have been claimed as 'Pictish' – metalwork andstones with Pictish symbols for example. It is, however, notable that these Pictish features are almost exclusively high-status. Mundane objects are remarkably uniform across Scotland north of the Forth–Clyde line, and were used and enjoyed by all the peoples, including the Scots. Therefore the term 'Pict' cannot be assumed to be specifically generic, racial, cultural or national. In our view it should probably be regarded as denoting a horizontal slice across the 'top' of society. The overwhelming evidence suggests that although the Roman authors can be read to refer to the Picts as though they were a tribal group or groups, it makes more sense to read the Pictish archaeological material as indicating a ruling class of certain Celtic tribes rather than of a total society.

Research suggests that there were many tribal groups in northern Scotland who, during the early centuries AD, grouped and re-grouped, partly in response to Rome, partly in response to their internal economic and social development, and we cannot really at this early period, or later, speak of a 'kingdom of the Picts'. The Pictish lands comprised many kingdoms with changing boundaries, and first one kingdom then another held supremacy over its neighbours. Interestingly, however, both the peoples of northern Scotland and their neighbours saw them as having some kind of underlying unity; they were known to the Irish as *Cruithni* – the word is related to the word *Pritani* or *Priteni*, from which the modern word 'Britain' is derived. The name might mean 'the people of shapes or designs', and again might be an allusion to tattooing. The Picts were believed to have been very long-established in Britain.

Although throughout northern Scotland continuity of population and traditions can be traced in archaeology from the Bronze Age (or even earlier) through to the time of the Picts, these traditions had regional differences which are perhaps reflected in some measure in the history of the Pictish kingdoms. We can recognize an Atlantic province, comprising the northern isles, the north Scottish mainland and the western highlands and islands. The landscape here in the Iron Age was dominated by different types of stone-walled forts, called 'brochs' and 'duns' by archaeologists. The western part of this region was taken over by the Scots. The second main region comprises the rest of the north Scottish mainland and is known as the north-eastern province. This lacked brochs, though it had some stone-walled forts of which the most characteristic, in the earlier part of the Iron Age at any rate, had timber-laced ramparts which were frequently fired and fused into a characteristic slaggy mass. These are known as 'vitrified forts'. Also in this region are to be found settlements with associated underground passages called 'souterrains', though these are also found (rather more rarely) in the Atlantic province.

Although the Atlantic province was certainly controlled by powerful chiefs in the Iron Age period of the broch builders (first century BC/ first century AD), it seems to have been less important in the early Middle Ages, when power was first strongest in the northern part of the north-eastern province, then subsequently in the southern part.

Among the neighbours of the Picts in early medieval times were the Irish, who, like other Celts, supported a plethora of kings, of varying ranks. The closest neighbour to Scotland was the region known as Ulster, and it was from here (though not exclusively) that raids were mounted on Roman Britain in the third and more particularly the fourth century AD.

The people known as the Scots came from a part of what is now County Antrim, known as 'Dalriada'. The name 'Scot' is an Irish one and means 'bandits', but was notably not given to them by the Romans or Britons on whom they preyed.

The factors behind the Irish raids and subsequent settlement are complex, involving both politics and economics. The outcome, however, was the settlement of Irish in western Britain, Wales, south-west England and Scotland. It was the settlement in western Scotland of Irish from Dalriada in the later fifth century AD, traditionally under Fergus mac Erc, that marked the formation of the kingdom of the Dalriadic Scots. They probably found much of the area under-populated and soon established control over Argyll and the adjacent isles. Given the long-established links between the peoples of Scotland and Ireland and their alliances against the Romans in the fourth century, the initial Dalriadic settlement is hardly surprising and need not have involved much hostility, if any. Indeed, they may have been invited to settle, for purposes of defence, as Vortigern is reported to have invited the Anglo-Saxons in fifth-century England. However, hostility grew between the Picts and Scots, even while their propinquity led to a cross-fertilization of ideas, particularly in the field of art: apparently a classic 'love–hate' relationship.

The Scots spoke a primitive Old Irish, and their settlement led in due course to the establishment of Scots Gaelic (which is an offshoot of Irish) in Scotland. The language of the Picts is lost to us, but seems to have been essentially a British Celtic language, distantly related to Welsh. Until the sixth century AD the history of both the Picts and the Scots is largely legendary, but from the arrival of Columba and the foundation of the monastery of Iona in Dalriada the documentary evidence becomes fuller and a little more reliable. The Picts were finally absorbed by the Scots in the ninth century AD under the leadership of the Dalriadic king, Kenneth mac Alpin, though the events leading up to this are obscure. Thereafter Picts and Scots formed a united kingdom of Alban, though undoubtedly local traditions lingered long.

The evidence for the Picts and Scots comprises documentary sources, most of which are Irish, a few Anglo-Saxon. Virtually none are native Pictish. Along with these can be set clues culled from personal and place-names. The archaeological evidence comprises a very large number of sculptured stones and much ornamental metalwork from Pictland, a few settlement sites and a scatter of graves. Of the settlements, Dunadd and Dunollie (in Dalriada), and Dundurn, Clatchard Craig and Burghead (in Pictland) are the most informative.

The Picts and Scots between them were responsible for some of the greatest art to survive from early medieval Europe. The cross-slabs of Pictland are masterpieces of sculpture, monuments such as the Nigg stone being 'manuscripts in stone' with a rich symbolic imagery, while the St Andrews Shrine is regarded by many as the finest early medieval sculpture surviving. If it is accepted that the Scots of Dalriada were responsible for the Book of Durrow and the Book of Kells, they can claim responsibility for two of the finest illuminated medieval manuscripts to have survived the ravages of time. Even if this is not accepted, it must be admitted that the Book of Kells was probably partly produced on Iona under Pictish influence. The ornamental metalwork of the Picts and Scots was no less accomplished, as shown by the St Ninian's Isle treasure. But perhaps the most interesting contribution of the Picts and Scots to archaeology was the repertoire of Pictish symbols incised on stone. Their meaning and date have still not been fully determined, but they remain an astonishing tribute to the ingenuity of these Dark Age peoples.

This book begins (Chapter 1) by looking at the Picts, and discusses what is known of their language and history, and their conversion to Christianity, tracing the remains of their churches and monasteries. Chapter 2 reviews the Scots, looking at them in their homelands then tracing their settlement in Dalriada and their subsequent history. The mission of Columba and the foundation of Iona provides a background to a survey of the early Christian remains of Dalriada. In Chapter 3 a discussion of what is known of the everyday life of the Picts and Scots from archaeology and from representations on sculptured stones is followed by a survey of the different types of settlement found in their territories. Chapter 4 is devoted to their art, in metal, in stone and in manuscript.

CHAPTER 1

The Picts

A twelfth-century Icelandic chronicler in the Historia Norvegiae described the Picts as pygmies who 'did wonders in the mornings and the evenings but at mid-day lost their strength and hid in holes in the ground'. The story is typical of medieval mythology, but it illustrates the fact that there was something about the Picts of which myths are made. Over the past two centuries, during which interest in the Picts has grown considerably, emphasis has been laid on the 'problem' of the Picts. Speculation has surrounded the interpretation of the symbols that appear incised on stone throughout Pictland, and debate has focused on which language the Picts must have spoken, since our main clues are surviving personal and place-names. If these were not mysteries enough, what is to be made of the unknown alphabet that appears on the Newton stone in Aberdeenshire, and why are the ogham inscriptions found in Pictland apparently gibberish? One scholar writing as late as the 1950s felt it necessary to say: 'It is a sad, if somewhat surprising, fact that we cannot with confidence affix the label 'Pictish' to a single dwelling or a single burial. . . . Which houses and which graves are Pictish? Where can we find them? And how can we recognize them?' (F.T. Wainwright, in *Problem of the Picts*, 1955). As we hope will be seen in this chapter, Pictish studies have come a long way from that *cri de coeur* in 1955, but the fact remains that we still do not know as much about the Picts as we perhaps feel we should.

Research has begun to clarify some facts about the Picts. For one thing, it is clear that the people to whom the term was given by Classical writers were the indigenous inhabitants of Scotland north of the Forth–Clyde line, whose origins are to be sought in the Iron Age and possibly even the Bronze Age in this part of Britain. What, politically, became Pictland in the early Middle Ages incorporated diverse groups of people with different cultural traditions, who at various times had allied and formed themselves into differing tribal groupings. Perhaps the arrival of the Scots in the western part of their former territories gave them a greater sense of identity than they had previously possessed. In any event, their Scottish neighbours had a considerable cultural impact on them, and by the ninth century AD caused them to disappear as a political entity under Scottish supremacy.

Sources for the study of the Picts are uneven: most of the documentary evidence for their history comes not from Pictland but from neighbouring areas, particularly Ireland, and at best is extremely scrappy and tantalizing. While of course shedding no light on politics and personalities, archaeology has been able to contribute some understanding of the economy, society and culture of the Picts. But even here the evidence is sparse, partly because much of the area has been untroubled by development, resulting in a scarcity of chance finds in urban building or large-scale roadworks.

Antiquaries and the Picts

Interest in the Picts started in the sixteenth century, when John White, famous for his drawings of American Indians on the Roanoke voyages of Sir Walter Raleigh in the period following 1584, attempted to draw them. For White the Pict was to be compared with a 'noble savage' from Barbary's farthest shore. Hector Boece, the sixteenth-century Scottish historian, commented on the Picts. To William Camden, the Elizabethan antiquary, too, they were simply wild savages from the pages of history who were partly instrumental in the break-up of Roman Britain. Camden, however, had some perceptive observations to make. He disputed Bede's statement that the Picts came from Scythia, and suggested that they were native Britons who had migrated north at the time of the Roman conquest. He believed them to be the same as the Caledonians, whom he saw as Britons, and had several observations to make about the name 'Pict' and Pictish tattooing. He wrote (here quoted from the 1695 edition of his *Britannia*, edited by Gibson):

> But for this name of the *Picts*, the authority of Flavius Vegetius will clear all doubts concerning it. He in some measure demonstrates, that the Britains us'd the word *Pictae* to express a thing coloured, in the very same sense that the Romans did. For he says that the Britains call'd your Scout-pinnaces Pictae, the sails and cables thereof being dy'd blue, and the mariners and soldiers clad in habits of the same colour. Certainly if the Britains would call ships from their sails of *blue-dye* Pictae, there is no reason in the world, why they should not give the name *Picti* to a people that painted their bodies with several colours, and especially with blue (for that is the dye that woad gives).

Little interest focused on trying to identify the remains of the Picts until the eighteenth century. At this time the Pictish sculptured stones attracted the attention of travellers and were singled out as tourist attractions in such works as Thomas Pennant's *Tour*, published in 1771, and the work of Francis Grose, the friend of Robert Burns, whose

Figure 1 Drawings of a male and female Pict (c. 1585). These are the work of the Elizabethan explorer John White, who was comparing them with the Roanoake Indians he had seen and drawn on his visit to North America. His drawings were based on information from classical sources (another drawing, not shown, illustrates a Pict holding a spear with a knobbed butt of the kind described by Cassius Dio) and depicted the Renaissance idea of the 'noble savage'. (Photos: Trustees of the British Museum)

Antiquities of Scotland appeared in 1789–91. Although such accounts drew attention to the stones, little attempt was made to comment on them and what light they might shed, if any, on the Picts.

It was not until the discovery of the treasure of Pictish silver from Norrie's Law, Fife, in about 1819, that a new chapter opened in the study of the Picts. In the account of the find, published by John Buist, the treasure was not associated with Picts, but he was able to see the connection between the symbols on some of the pieces and the designs on stones.

The study was taken further with the publication of John Stuart's *The Sculptured Stones of Scotland*, in two volumes in 1856 and 1867. The connection was now firmly made between the stones and the Picts, and many important monuments were illustrated with beautiful engravings. From now on, new discoveries of stones were rapidly reported, and all the known finds were gathered together by Romilly Allen and Joseph Anderson in their monumental *Early Christian Monuments of Scotland*, published in 1903. Somewhat earlier, in 1881, Joseph Anderson had published two surveys of the remains of Scotland in the time of the Picts and Scots, *Scotland in Early Christian Times*, which still remain an important starting point for any study of their archaeology.

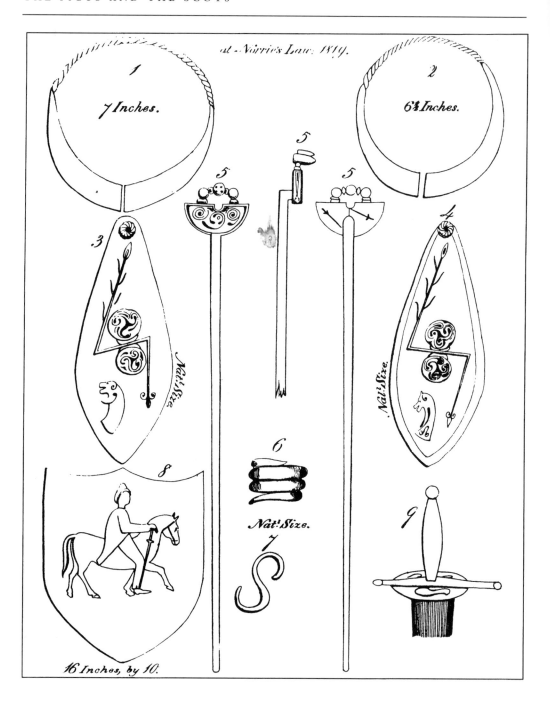

at Norrie's Law. 1819.

1

7 Inches.

2

6¼ Inches.

3

Nat¹ Size.

4

Nat¹ Size.

5

5

5

8

6

Nat¹ Size.

7

9

16 Inches, by 10.

Finding the Picts

The Picts' first documentary appearance was in Classical literature, in a panegyric by the writer Eumenius set down in AD 297. This has led some strict historians to decide that the Picts cannot have existed before this time. However, the text has survived only by chance – if we had no work by Eumenius, the next reference to the Picts would takes us to the fourth century, by which time the Picts were well established. It seems more reasonable to assume that by the time of Eumenius the term 'Pict' was well known enough not to require explanation to an educated Mediterranean readership. Since there is no evidence of direct Roman conflict with the northern barbarians after the time of Septimius Severus at the beginning of that century, it is a reasonable but unprovable guess that the term came into fashion in the time of Severus' campaigns. Regardless of when they were so named, the Picts are clearly the same stock as earlier inhabitants of northern Scotland, since there is no archaeological or other evidence for incomers in this region on any scale in later prehistory. It is this fact that leads to the conclusion that this is political, ethnic and/or linguistic nomenclature rather than genetic or racial.

Cassius Dio, another Classical writer, recorded that there were two tribes in northern Scotland in the early third century, the *Caledonii* and *Maeatae*. The Verona List of AD 313 seems to replace *Maeatae* with Picts when it refers to 'Picts and Caledonians', but we would probably be wrong to infer from this that only *Maeatae* were Picts, for in 310 reference was already being made to 'Caledonians and other Picts'. The sixth-century Ravenna Cosmography mentions 'Pexa' in a list of the forts of the Antonine Wall. This was clearly based on old information (the Antonine Wall did not survive into the third century) and it has been suggested that the Pexa is a scribal error for *Pecti* or *Pectia*, and is in fact a reference to Picts around the area of the Antonine Wall.

The Classical sources seem to indicate, therefore, that the Picts comprised at least two main tribal groups, who were discernible in Scotland from the beginning of the third century until the fourth. Of the two groups, the Caledonians were active in the time of Agricola, the late first-century Roman general who campaigned in Scotland, while the *Maeatae* are not mentioned until AD 197–200, when they attacked the Romans, and the Caledonians are reported as breaking promises to aid them.

As far as can be established, the *Maeatae* were situated in the region immediately behind the Antonine Wall and the Caledonians further north. The *Maeatae* have perhaps left their tribal name in the modern place-names Dumyat and Myot Hill in Stirlingshire.

The two-fold division of the peoples living in northern Scotland seems to have survived into later times. The *Maeatae* may be the same as the *Miathi* mentioned by Adomnan as engaged in a battle in north-eastern Strathmore, probably the Battle of Circind. Somewhat earlier there are

Figure 2 (opposite) Drawing of some of the finds from the hoard of Pictish silver found at Norrie's Law, Fife. This was published by John Buist in 1838. The drawings are clearly very inaccurate. The sword pommel is probably an imaginative interpretation since it appears to depict a later medieval broadsword. The shield with a mounted figure may have been a votive plaque, the figure copied from the stone from Largo which was probably originally associated with the Norrie's Law deposit. Some of these items survive

Roman references to *Dicalydones* and *Verturiones* as representing the two main division of Picts (*Dicalydones* in itself implies a bipartite division). Bede wrote of northern and southern Picts as two distinct groups in the seventh century.

What all this seems to reveal is that from early in the first millennium AD there were two main groups of peoples in northern Scotland, perhaps encompassing smaller tribal divisions, and that the term 'Pict' came to be applied to them by the Romans, perhaps from the second century AD onwards. Various factors, including the threat of Rome, may have led to increasing unity among the northern peoples, which gave them the strength in the fourth century for their campaigns against the Romans.

All of the foregoing inference and information derives from Roman sources, but what have other commentators to add, and what have the Picts to say for themselves? The evidence comprises (a) the language and inscriptions left by the Picts themselves, (b) Dark Age and later medieval literary references set down in Ireland and elsewhere, and (c) archaeology – the clues provided by the forts and farms, the pottery and the metalwork. The evidence often conflicts or appears not to correlate, adding to the elusive quality of these ancestors of modern Scotland, and reinforcing our conviction that the term was too loosely used in antiquity to have real meaning in terms of the archaeological record that now exists.

Historical Sources for the Picts

The study of the Picts is made difficult because of the lack of documentary sources, and also because the native language of the Picts is lost. These two facts are in some measure interrelated, insofar as the loss of the Pictish language came about through its replacement by Scots Gaelic. When people no longer spoke Pictish, they were not inclined to transcribe texts in an obsolete language. The dearth of Pictish documentary sources is partly explained by the fact that recording within Pictland was probably carried out by monks in the seventh century and later, who would have written in Latin. The conversion to Christianity probably influenced strongly both the language and the thought of people in Pictland. Also, the adoption of Latin as the medium for writing was called for, as shown by the Christian Latin formula on a sword chape from the treasure from St Ninian's Isle, Shetland, inscribed 'IN NOMINE D[EI] S[UMMI]': 'In the Name of God the Highest'.

Another obstacle in studying the Picts is that very few original 'Dark Age' documents from any part of Britain have survived; most of the existing texts are copies made in the twelfth century or later, prompted by an antiquarian fascination in the past. The conquering Scots fostered no such interest in Pictish history, so copies were probably made only rarely. There are relatively few surviving documentary sources for the history of the Scots prior to the later eleventh century either, so it seems very probable that Latin texts were destroyed partly through Edward I removing Scottish records to London in the thirteenth century (where they were not cared for), and perhaps also because of the destruction of archives in Scottish monasteries in the Reformation of the sixteenth century.

Most information about Pictish history therefore comes from Roman records and other external sources. The most important of these sources are the Irish Annals – year-by-year records of events set down initially to facilitate remembering particular years for the calculation of the date of Easter. Two such collections provide useful data on Pictish history, the Annals of Tigernach and the Annals of Ulster. It has been argued, convincingly, that the Pictish material incorporated in both was derived from a now-lost collection of Annals set down on Iona. These records appear to have dated back from before c. 750, when the Annals were first compiled from older material. After 750 the references to Scotland are less frequent in the Irish Annals, which now appear to have been updated in Ireland rather than drawing upon an Iona source. After 750, references to Dalriada are relatively sparse in the Irish Annals, but between c. 760 and 840 there is more information relating to the Picts, perhaps indicating that information was derived at that period from a source in Pictland – Dr Isabel Henderson has suggested the monastery of Applecross in Ross.

In addition to the Irish material there is a native source but, alas, it is no more informative than a list of kings. Two versions of the Pictish king list survive. One is a very late and distorted copy. The other was collected together with other sources on early Scottish history in a fourteenth-century volume in Paris, known as the Latin Ms 4126. The Pictish king list appears alongside a Scottish Chronicle in the book, and it has been suggested that both are derived from an original tenth-century source. The Pictish king list gives the names in Pictish form, a fact that has helped linguists to work out which language the Picts spoke.

In addition to these sources, it is possible to draw on references in the work of other writers, such as the Venerable Bede, and Adomnan in his Life of Columba, for supporting information.

The Picts in History

The first documentary evidence of the Picts was the result of Roman contact with the northern tribes. The story of the Roman impact on northern Scotland may go back to the time of the kings of the Orkneys, who seem to have sent ambassadors to Claudius at the time of the conquest of Britain in AD 43. The Roman advance into Britain took until AD 82–90 to reach the Forth–Clyde line, when Agricola established a series of forts before advancing northwards. Agricola marched into northern Scotland and fought a decisive victory over the

Figure 3 The Mither Tap of Bennachie from Durno, Aberdeenshire. This is probably where the Roman forces under Agricola met the Caledonians in the battle of Mons Graupius in AD 84. (Photo: Jim Henderson)

Caledonians, who were led by Calgacus, at Mons Graupius. In the eighteenth century this battle gave its name to the Grampian Mountains, owing to a belief at that time that it was fought there. It is not known where it was fought, but a plausible suggestion is that it may have been located near the Iron Age fort of Bennachie in Aberdeenshire – not far away is an exceptionally large Roman marching camp at Durno, which could have been the gathering point for the Roman troops. The Caledonians had long swords and chariots, and numbered thirty thousand men. Their tactics were unsuited to success when fighting an efficient military machine like the Roman army.

Agricola built marching camps on Strathmore, and what were to have been permanent forts at Strathcathro and Inchtuthil, Perthshire. The latter fort was to have been a legionary base, but in AD 86, before it was finished, problems on the Danube resulted in the troops being pulled out of Britain, and Inchtuthil was dismantled.

After this brief interlude the north was left to its own devices. The Forth–Clyde line seems to have become the northern frontier of Britannia. The Antonine Wall was built here by Antoninus Pius in AD 142. It measured forty Roman miles in length, and cut off the ancestral Picts from the South. The Antonine Wall was held until soon after the death of Pius in 161, then the military frontier was moved back southwards to the line of Hadrian's Wall, between the Tyne and Solway. The Antonine Wall forts were briefly put back into use during the second century as needs dictated.

The later second century was a time of turmoil for northern Britain. Around 180 the northern tribes 'crossed the wall that separated them from the Roman forts, did a great deal of damage, and cut down a general and his troops'. These are the words of Cassius Dio. A new governor was installed in Britain and order was restored, but not for long. At the end of the century the uprising of the Caledonians and *Maeatae* took place. On that occasion the northern tribes were bought off by the governor of Britain 'for a great sum', but it was clearly not enough to buy peace for long. In 208 the governor of Britannia was forced to appeal to the emperor for help, and Septimius Severus, a veteran campaigner, decided to come in person with his sons, Caracalla and Geta, and a suitably large army. Part of his objective was to toughen up his sons into seasoned fighters. Campaigning began in 209 and the northern tribes were rapidly brought to heel. But in 210 there was a revolt, and Severus, lying ill at York, sent Caracalla to deal with it and kill everyone the army met (an instruction dear to Caracalla's heart). Severus died at York in 211, and Caracalla abandoned the conquest of the North, returning in haste to Rome to take up his destiny as emperor.

For the rest of the third century, Hadrian's Wall was the frontier of the province. If there was trouble from the northern tribesmen there is no record of it, and it is not until records of the fourth century that the Picts appear on the scene in full force, with historical 'identity tags'.

The Pictish Wars

The fourth century opened with a period of trouble from the northern tribes. In 305–6, Constantius Chlorus campaigned against the 'Caledonians and other Picts'. In 315, Constantine the Great assumed the title of 'Britannicus Maximus', perhaps bestowed on him because of successful campaigns in the North. In 343 his son Constans engaged in a campaign against the Picts, as well as the *areani* (or *arcani*) who seem to have been northern spies. A peace treaty may have followed, since an agreement was reported as having been broken in 360 when Picts, now allied with Scots of Ireland, harried the frontier areas and appear to have been driven back.

The aggression was building up and was becoming more intense and frequent. In 364–5 the Roman historian, Ammianus Marcellinus, identified *Dicalydones*, *Verturiones*, Scots, *Attacotti* and Saxons for the first time. These tribes caused problems on all Britain's frontiers. To what extent they were working in collusion is not clear – the Saxon raids on the South are unlikely to have been connected. It is equally unclear

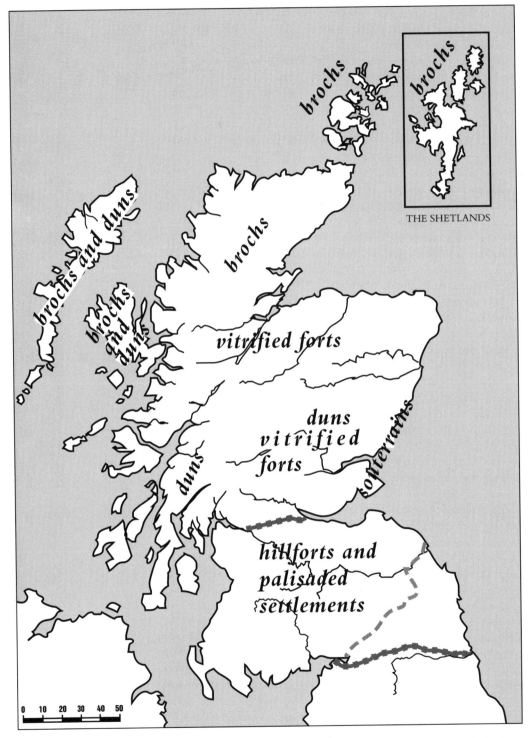

THE SHETLANDS

Figure 4 Iron Age Scotland.
Scale is in miles

what relationship these peoples had to one another: were the *Dicalydones* a restructuring of the *Caledonii*, and, if so, does that imply they had been split? Also, what had happened to the *Maeatae*? We are left to ponder, with no answers.

In 367–9, however, the Picts allied with Scots and *Attacotti* in a 'barbarian conspiracy'. Count Theodosius was sent to Britain and put the province to rights. Peace lasted little more than ten years. In 382 Picts and Scots invaded Britannia and were driven back by Magnus Maximus. Finally in 396–8 there was yet another raid on the province by the Picts, this time repulsed by the general Stilicho.

The extent of these northern barbarian raids is difficult to estimate. Political motives may have led to the raids being blown up out of all proportion to the damage they caused, as may be the case with the Conspiratio Barbarica of 367. What cannot, however, be doubted is that the northern tribes in the fourth century pursued an ongoing policy of harrying Roman Britain. Why?

There is no clear answer to the above question, but two possibilities come to mind. First, the Picts and their allies saw Roman Britain as a source of desirable commodities. At the end of the second century they had been paid off, and no doubt felt they could do with more of the same treatment. This may have happened during the third century, but failed to attract comment from Roman writers since it would have shown the Romans in a poor light as having to resort to bribery. When these inducements were not forthcoming, the Picts may have headed south to take what they wanted instead.

There is some evidence that Roman silver was reaching northern Scotland in appreciable quantities in the third and fourth centuries. It has been suggested that a hoard of coins found at Falkirk, Stirlingshire, had been put together in Scotland prior to AD 230, accumulated by a barbarian leader out of subsidies received from the Romans over a long period. Four further hoards from south-east Pictland have been equated with a move in the time of Septimus Severus to buy peace. It is true that there are few later stray finds of high-denomination Roman coins in Scotland, though Aberdeenshire has yielded two gold and one silver coin of the fourth century. But much of the silver coming into Scotland was probably melted down and subsequently found its way into Dark Age hoards of silverwork, such as those from Norrie's Law, Fife, and Gaulcross, Banff, or into the silver chains that analysis has suggested were, sometimes at least, made from melted-down Roman silver plate (see p. 112 and p. 114, respectively). In addition, the spectacular hoard of late Roman silverwork, including Christian pieces, from Traprain Law, East Lothian, may be connected with Pictish looting or Roman buy-offs, even though this site lies just outside historical Pictland. Silver seems to have been the metal most favoured for ornamental metalworking in Pictland, and it is difficult to see from where silver was obtained if not from surviving stocks of Roman metalwork. Even as late as the eighth century, Roman models may have been

Figure 5 Detail from the
Bridgeness slab, found in 1868,
showing a Roman riding down
barbarians. It records the
construction of about 6.6 km of
the Antonine Wall by troops
from the second legion. (Photo:
© The Trustees of the National
Museums of Scotland)

Figure 6 Some items from the Traprain treasure, found on the site of a hillfort in East Lothian in the early twentieth century. The hoard seems to have been in the process of being broken up for scrap. The silver plate, which came from Gaul and probably Britain, included some pieces with Christian subject-matter and items from the territory of the Goths. It may have been loot, but it could equally have been part of a buy-off of northern tribes. (Photo: Royal Museums of Scotland)

available to inspire some of the suspiciously Roman-looking features of the St Ninian's Isle treasure (see p. 145).

A second possibility is connected with population expansion and political upheaval in northern Scotland itself. This will be discussed later (see p. 81).

The Pictish Wars can be viewed from an angle other than that of the Romans. Some documentary evidence from Dark Age sources sheds light on the wars. The Picts are first mentioned in a native fifth-century source: St Patrick's Letter to the Soldiers of Coroticus, a king of south-west Scotland. Patrick had a low opinion of them, calling them 'most shameful, wicked, and apostate Picts', implying that at some stage during their brushes with Rome in the fourth century, some at least had been converted to Christianity. They receive an equally bad press from the monk Gildas. Writing in *c.* 540, he is well known for the forthright and somewhat over-theatrical phraseology he used. The Picts clearly stimulated raw emotions in him: for him they were the 'foul hordes of Scots and Picts, like dark throngs of worms who wriggle out of narrow fissures in the rock when the sun is high and the weather grows warm'. Gildas gave an account of three Pictish Wars: the first was that of 382–90, the incursion repulsed by Magnus Maximus (independently mentioned by the 'Gallic Chronicler'); the second was repulsed by

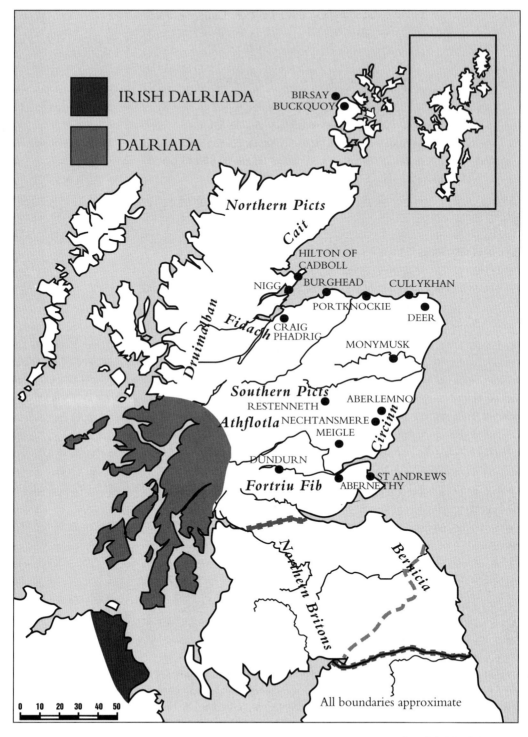

Figure 7 Historical Pictland.
Scale is in miles

Stilicho (independently attested by the historian Claudian); the third occurred in the 450s. Gildas recounted that at the time of this third war the Britons appealed to 'Agitius Thrice Consul', who is usually identified with Aetius, consul for the third time in 446. Aetius died in 454, so the defeat of the Picts and the end of this war can probably be fixed somewhere in the 450s. This appears to have been the last time the Picts and Scots were acting as allies, though Gildas implied that the Scots went back to Ireland with the intention of soon returning.

Thus far the earliest appearances of the Picts in documentary history as enemies of Rome have been traced. The period of the late fifth and sixth centuries is one of comparative historical darkness in Pictland. Apart from the backward-looking comments of Gildas, all that exist are the names of some Pictish kings in a king list, which are corrupt if not fictitious for this period.

The first historical personage in the king list was Bridei mac Maelcon, whose accession took place *c.* 550. According to Adomnan, Bridei played an important role in the conversion of the Picts to Christianity. Bridei's father Maelcon had a Welsh name, and may have been Maelgwn, King of Gwynedd. Maelgwn was much hated by Gildas and was said to have been descended from Cunedda, a ruler of the region around the Firth of Forth who migrated to Wales near the end of the fourth century or the beginning of the fifth. Maelgwn was the most reviled of all Gildas' victims: 'What of you, dragon of the island? . . . You are last in my list, but first in evil . . . Why wallow like a fool in the ancient ink of your crimes, like a man drunk on wine pressed from the vine of the Sodomites?'

Bridei may not have been as steeped in evil as Gildas believed Maelgwn to be, but he was a strong and dynamic leader in Pictland. He defeated the Scots and established a peace between the two peoples for fifteen years. Adomnan's account of Columba's mission to the Picts is clouded by hagiographical convention, but he located Bridei's stronghold near the River Ness, and Craig Phadrig has been claimed as the site. Adomnan said that Bridei had hostages from the King of Orkney, who was at his court at the time, implying a system of sub-kings under Bridei's control. He also said that Bridei ruled both Northern and Southern Picts.

The end of Bridei's reign may have been taken up with troubles in southern Pictland. Bridei is recorded as having died in the Battle of Asreth in Circinn, which seems to have happened in 584. It may have been that power shifted after this battle from the northern to the southern Picts. After the Battle of Degsastan in 603, when Aethelfrith the King of Northumbria defeated Aedan of the Scots, working perhaps in alliance with the Britons of Strathclyde, Scottic dreams of power in regions to their south were curtailed. Instead, the Scots had to focus their ambitions on Pictland, and hostilities were resumed. Aethelfrith extended Northumbrian territory as far as the Firth of Forth, so that southern Picts and Anglo-Saxons now found themselves neighbours.

One can only surmise what was happening in Pictland during the first half of the seventh century. There were probably skirmishes with the Scots, but the strongest threat to Pictish independence came from the Northumbrians on their southern border. At first contact between the two peoples seems to have been positive and peaceable. Northumbria was divided between Deira in the south and Bernicia in the North, and south-east Scotland was part of Bernicia also. The ruler of Deira triumphed over the Bernicians, and in 617 the sons of the Bernician ruler Aethelfrith were exiled. Some went to Ireland and some to Pictland, where one, Eanfrith, married a Pictish princess. The king of Deira was however killed, and Eanfrith went back to rule Bernicia, only to be killed himself soon after on a visit to Mercia.

Oswald succeeded Eanfrith as ruler of Northumbria, uniting Bernicia and Deira. His brother Oswiu extended Northumbrian territory with the conquest of part of Dalriada and Pictland. Bede, the main source of information, does not describe how or even when this came about, but it is assumed to have happened around 668. It would seem that the victory over Dalriada did not extend to occupation, only to the exacting of tribute. In southern Pictland, however, it was otherwise, and it is likely that much of the area was held by the Northumbrians for a while, though it has also been argued that their holdings were mainly confined to Fife. Free Pictland was ruled by a certain Gartnait and his successor Drest. The southern Picts were controlled by the Angles for thirty years.

The Life of St Wilfrid suggests that all was not peaceful among the northern Picts. Drest seems to have stirred up a revolt with the intention of driving out the Northumbrians from the South, but his bid for victory led instead to disaster. Ecgfrith of Northumbria crushed the revolt. He is said to have made a bridge of Pictish corpses over two rivers, so that his army could cross without getting their feet wet and wipe out the rest of the Pictish army.

Drest was deposed in 672, and his successor was Bridei mac Bili. Bridei mac Bili appears to have campaigned widely and successfully, mustering a fleet and destroying the growing power of the Orkneys in 682. No doubt surrounds Bridei's leadership at Nechtansmere in 685. In this battle, fought probably near Dunnichen in Angus, Bridei defeated Ecgfrith on 20 May 685. Ecgfrith was killed and his trapped army massacred.

Of the Northumbrians remaining in Pictland, many were killed or enslaved. All Pictish territory was reclaimed and Bridei ruled over Pictland for eight years until his death in 693.

The next landmark in Pictish history is the reign of Nechton mac Derelei, who succeeded to the throne of Pictland in 706. Nechton can be credited with ending the conflict with Northumbria and opening up Pictland to Anglian influence. He sought advice from Northumbria on ecclesiastical matters, and as a result the Picts thenceforward followed Northumbria and therefore the Roman Church in the matter of the

Figure 8 Detail from the back of the Aberlemno churchyard cross. This has been seen as representing the Battle of Nechtansmere, which was fought successfully by the Picts against the Anglo-Saxons of Northumbria in 685, probably at Dunnichen Moss, not far from Aberlemno. The scene shows a dead warrior (probably an Anglo-Saxon), in what appears to be chain-mail, being pecked by a crow or raven. (Photo: RCAHMS)

method of calculating Easter. He introduced Northumbrian masons to provide guidance in the building of churches.

His reign, however, was not without misfortune. His brother Ciniod was murdered by the King of Atholl, and Nechton retaliated by imprisoning the king. This put an end to internal problems for a period of ten years, but Nechton abdicated in 724 to enter a monastery. His abdication may not have been entirely voluntary, and his sucessor, Drust, was deposed in 726 by Alpin. This rapid succession reveals a period of turmoil in Pictland and a scrabble for the throne. In the end, Alpin was no more successful in holding the throne than his predecessors, and the ultimate victor was Oengus (Onuist or Angus) mac Fergus.

Oengus' rise to supremacy came at the end of a series of battles between 728 and 729. In the final showdown of 729, Oengus fought first Nechton at Monith Carno, and then killed Drust at Cath Droma Deirg Blathuug. Oengus was thus already a hardened campaigner when he succeeded to the Pictish throne.

Oengus' first target was now Dalriada. Here he campaigned vigorously for a number of years, during which he may have extended the theatre of war to Ireland. By 741 he had gained control over Dalriada and was ready to turn his attention to the powerful British kingdom of Alt Clut, Strathclyde.

Throughout the period of campaigning against the Scots, relations between Picts and Northumbrians had remained fairly peaceful, though in 740 an unsuccessful attempt was made by Eadberht of Northumbria to invade southern Pictland while Oengus was preoccupied with Dalriada. It was not successful, and Eadberht found that Aethelbald of Mercia was playing the same game, invading Northumbria while the Northumbrian king was absent in Pictland.

In 750, Oengus now apparently allied with Cuthred of Wessex and Aethelbald of Mercia against the Strathclyde Britons, but the alliance seems to have fallen apart because Cuthred fell out with the other two. The Britons retaliated against the Picts who, under the leadership of Talorcan, Oengus' brother, were defeated. Talorcan was killed in battle. Weakened by this disaster, Oengus allied with Northumbria in 756 and advanced on Alt Clut, Dumbarton Rock. At first it looked as though they were going to be successful, but a reverse of fortune wiped out the invading army. Oengus retreated to Pictland to die in 761.

Once again a blanket of silence covers the ensuing events. Dalriada won back its independence from the Picts under Aed Finn, son of Eochaid, some time before 778. The fortunes of both peoples fluctuated through the latter years of the eighth century and into the opening years of the ninth. It is therefore exasperating for historians that the events leading up to the conquest of Pictland by Kenneth mac Alpin, King of the Scots, in 843 or 844, are unrecorded. It is not, however, as mysterious as it used to appear. As has been pointed out, Kenneth was not the first king to rule over Picts and Scots together – no less than three Scottish kings had ruled over Pictland for a time, and as early as the beginning of the eighth century some Pictish kings had Gaelic names which betray a Dalriadic origin. At the beginning of the ninth century, Constantine, son of Fergus, figured both as a ruler of Dalriada and of the Picts (who knew him as Castantin son of Uurguist). His successor, the Dalriadic ruler Oengus II, appeared in Pictland as Unuist son of Uurguist, and his son, Eoganan (or Uen), ruled over both Picts and Scots until his death in 839. Since these rulers appear to have been of Dalriadic origin, though ruling Pictland from Forteviot, inside Pictish territory, it might be guessed that the Scots had in the early ninth century pushed eastwards into Pictland. Kenneth's final triumph over the Picts was probably no more than the culmination of a long period of growing Dalriadic control, helped by the threat of the Norse to Pictish territories. In 839 the people of Fortriu (or Fortrenn, an area on the upper waters of the Earn and the Forth) were defeated by the Vikings, and among the dead numbered two sons of the Pictish king Oengus. It provided an opportunity for Kenneth mac Alpin to take over. Nothing is known about Alpin, Kenneth's father, and it is likely that Kenneth fought his way from an obscure background to gain control of both Scots and Picts.

The Language of the Picts

Information about the lost language of the Picts is scanty and tantilizing. The king list may be the most useful source, giving as it does the names of kings in Pictish form, but it is not the only one; there are in addition place-names and a small number of inscriptions from Pictland.

The Pictish inscriptions are in three alphabets: ogham, which was invented in Ireland, perhaps around the fourth century, and introduced to Scotland via Dalriada; insular, which similarly reached the Picts via Dalriada; and an unknown script represented in only one inscription on a stone at Newton, Aberdeenshire.

The Newton stone's inscription was first noticed in 1803 when it stood beside the road at Shevack, Aberdeenshire. Along the edge of the stone is further writing in ogham. The main inscription was first transcribed by the Earl of Southesk, and a succession of commentators have attempted to read it, with astonishing results: Gaelic, Latin, Greek and even Phoenician have been proposed as the source of the language! It has been suggested that it was a nineteenth-century forgery, but careful examination of the weathering of the lettering showed that it was contemporaneous with the ogham inscription which has been dated to the seventh or eighth century. The likeliest explanation for the mysterious inscription is that it was carved in imitation of Irish majuscule script by someone who was illiterate. A recent but as yet unproven suggestion is that the letters correspond to a Continental manuscript hand of the fifth

Figure 9 The Newton stone, Aberdeenshire. Long-suspected of being a nineteenth-century forgery on account of the unique lettering that appears on it, this stone has been shown to have been carved in the same way as other Pictish engravings. The bilingual inscription is equally unintelligible in both the mystery script and in the ogham alphabet. It probably dates from the eighth century and possibly represents an attempt to write by someone who was illiterate. (Photo: Kathy Parker)

Figure 10 Transcript of the Newton stone inscription. (Drawing: L. Laing)

century AD. The inscription may be a translation of the ogham, which has been deciphered and appears to include the personal name Eddarrnonn.

Of the eight non-ogham texts, five are in Latin and the others may have been but are not sufficiently legible. As well as containing Latin words, the inscriptions include personal names: Drosten, Uoret and Forcus (all on the Drosten stone at St Vigeans); Resad and Spusscio (if the reading is correct, on a sword chape from the St Ninian's Isle treasure); and -eton, which may be Pictish (at Barnakill). All except Forcus (which is Irish) are thought to be Pictish. The Drosten stone also has the word *ipe* which may mean either 'son of' or, more probably, 'and'.

The ogham inscriptions from Pictland are mostly found on stones, but there are in addition a few on other objects, including a knife-handle from Bac Mhic Connain in the Hebrides, a spindle whorl from Buckquoy, Orkney, a knife-handle from Aikerness, Orkney, and another, isolated, knife-handle from Weeting, Norfolk. The Pictish ogham alphabet started out closely following the Irish, but as time went on the Picts used more ornate forms and abandoned the edge of the stone in favour of drawing the guideline on the face of the stone instead. Only two Pictish stones (one of them the Newton stone) follows the Irish convention. The earliest could date from the fifth or sixth century, but most seem to be of the eighth.

The ogham inscriptions appear to be in Pictish, an assumption based on the fact that they are largely indecipherable. A stone from Lunnasting, Shetland, for example, reads: *ettocuhetts ahehhttannn hccevv nehhtons*. The last word is the name *Nehton*, which is a common Pictish personal name (see p. 17). The rest of the inscription is apparently meaningless, though it is just possible that the multiple consonant endings are plurals, following convention on Roman inscriptions where the last letter of an abbreviated title was multiplied to indicate the number involved, thus *AVGGG* stood for 'three Augusti'. Now and again a word that seems to be of Irish derivation appears in the inscriptions, such as *meqq*, which may be the same as the genitive form of the Irish *maqq*, meaning 'son of'. One ogham inscription from Bressay, Shetland, has both the word *crosscc*, which has been read as the Irish word for 'cross', and another, *dattrr*, which is thought to be the Norse for 'daughter'.

The last clue to the Pictish language is provided by place-names, the most important of which incorporate the element 'Pit-', as, for example, in Pitlochry and Pittenweem. The word is derived from 'pett', apparently meaning a parcel of land, and Pit- place-names are found all over the territories of the Picts. These place-names are 'Gallo-Brittonic' Celtic, though of an unusual form, and other Gallo-Brittonic Celtic names are found in Pictland. From this, Professor. Kenneth Jackson deduced that place-names suggest that people in Pictland spoke a Brittonic (i.e. Gallo-Brittonic) Celtic language, but that it differed from the Brittonic Celtic dialect spoken south of the Forth–Clyde line. He argued that the personal names comprise a mixture of Brittonic Celtic and non-Celtic elements, and his conclusion was that the Picts spoke a basically Brittonic language, with elements derived from an older, non-Celtic speech.

Subsequent research has travelled some way towards refining Jackson's original interpretation. First, the Celtic element in Pictish seems quite closely related to Cumbric, the language spoken in north-west England. Second, a series of place-name elements – *carden, pert,*

Figure 11 Inscription on a panel at the bottom of the edge of the slab known as the Drosten stone (or St Vigeans No. 1), Angus. The inscription reads: *Drosten/ ipeuoret/ett for/cus*, in Irish letters. *Drosten* is a Pictish name, more familiar to us in the form of Tristan from medieval Arthurian romance. *Uoret* and *Forcus* are also personal names. (Photo: Scottish Development Department)

Figure 12 Both sides of a red deer antler knife-handle, probably eighth century. The handle bears a Pictish ogham inscription. It was found at Weeting, Norfolk. The inscription has not been deciphered satisfactorily. (Photo: Norfolk Museums Service)

lanerc, pevr and *aber* – mostly seem to relate to woodland. Third, place-names combine Brittonic Celtic with Goidelic Celtic (i.e. Gaelic) elements. This might suggest that in the seventh and eighth centuries when these names seem to have been formed, there was some degree of bilingualism in Pictland.

What does this tell us about the Picts? Celtic languages fall into two main groups: Goidelic Celtic, including Irish, Scots Gaelic and Manx, which are in general terms more 'primitive' (i.e. complex and earlier); and Brittonic Celtic, which are generally more evolved and include Welsh, Cornish and Cumbric. It would appear that an early form of Brittonic Celtic was spoken in Iron Age and native Roman Britain. Out of this, Welsh, for example, evolved in the fifth century. Since Celtic is now seen by many as evolving over a long period of time in several parts of Europe, it is possible that the non-Celtic element in Pictish reflects a language spoken earlier in prehistoric north-east Scotland, though this is, of course, beyond proof.

The Pagan Picts

Of the religion of the pagan Picts, virtually nothing is known, but it is fairly certain that in general terms their beliefs would have fallen into line with those of other pagan Celtic peoples. Almost certainly they had a great diversity of deities, including local ones which would have presided over rivers, lochs, forests, mountains and even trees. These would have been associated in some cases with particular animals, and certain animals too would have been regarded as sacred. These 'sacred' animals of the pre-Christian Picts probably comprised or included those that appear on the incised Pictish symbol stones. The large number of bulls carved on stones found at Burghead, Moray, might suggest that there was some kind of bull-cult there.

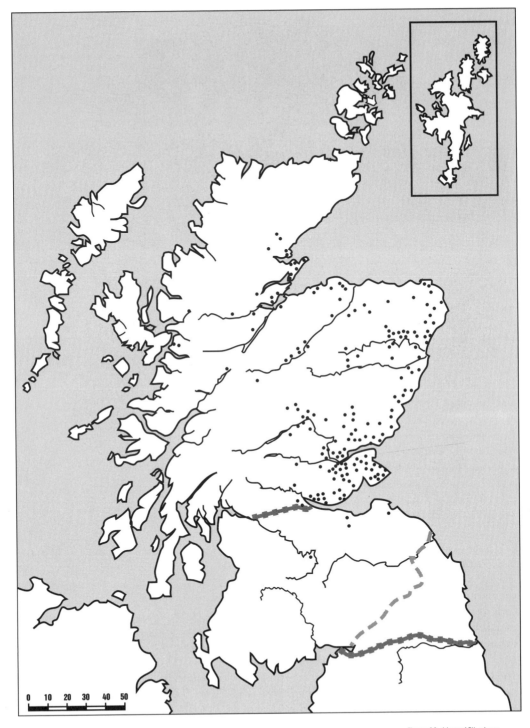

Figure 13 Map of Pit-place-names. Scale is in miles. (After Wainwright, with additions)

Figure 14 Carving of a bull, Burghead, Moray. There is a considerable number of such carvings from this site. Their appearance in isolation, without other Pictish symbols, suggests that their function was not the same as the symbol groups that appear on other stones in Pictland. There may have been a pagan bull cult at Burghead. (Photo: David Longley)

Human sacrifice (either by drowning or beheading) is suggested by the finds in the cave at Covesea, Moray (see p. 108). In addition, Pictish sculptures of the Christian period show such subject matter as a tree decorated with human heads, and a man being dropped head-first into a cauldron. The latter might have represented either sacrifice or rebirth: cauldrons figure prominently in Celtic legend. Some of the puzzling scenes on Christian Pictish stones may refer to pagan myths. A newly discovered slab from Shetland shows a man with a wolf mask, perhaps in a ceremony. Caves may have served as cult centres (for example Covesea or the caves at East Wemyss, Fife), while the occurrence of Pictish finds on earlier prehistoric ritual sites might imply a continuing reverence for old religious centres. The Gaulcross hoard, for example (see p. 113), was found in a prehistoric stone circle, and the well at Burghead, Moray, though later used by Christians, may have been a pagan cult centre.

The Pictish Church

Bede and Adomnan are the key sources for understanding the beginnings of Christianity in Pictland. Bede reported that the southern Picts were converted through the activities of St Ninian, and that the northern Picts first heard of Christ through the mission of St Columba to Bridei mac Maelcon. The last event is corroborated by Adomnan who, in his Life of Columba, gives a clear picture of the saint's visit to the court of Bridei, where he had to compete with a 'magus', a pagan priest called Broichan. Although Adomnan makes it clear that a couple of Pictish families were converted after the mission, he does not say that Bridei was, and as he is likely to have noted so important a conversion, we can probably assume that Bridei remained a pagan while showing respect for the Christian missionary.

The mission of St Ninian to the southern Picts has independent testimony provided by a probably eighth-century account of the saint's miracles, the Miracula Nynie Episcopi. This reports that Ninian converted the Picts after his return from Rome, which confirms Bede's description of him as a British bishop 'who had been regularly instructed at Rome'. The traditional view of Ninian was that he was a fifth-century figure, sent out perhaps from Carlisle to minister to an already Christian community at Whithorn in Galloway. Later legends make him a contemporary of St Martin of Tours, but there is no reason to believe this; indeed there is no reason either to assume a fifth-century date for the saint. Current excavations at Whithorn are bringing to light the remains of an early ecclesiastical foundation which was certainly in existence by the sixth century, if not before, but Ninian's date cannot be determined, though presumably he was the founder of this community.

Here the text in St Patrick's Letter to the Soldiers of Coroticus becomes important, since Patrick, writing in the fifth century, spoke of the 'apostate Picts'. To be apostate they must have been converted at some time, suggesting that some Picts were Christian in the fifth century or even the fourth. The likeliest contenders for this description are the southern Picts living to the north of the Firth of Forth. If their territory extended south of the Forth, which is not impossible in the later fourth or early fifth century, they might well have been converted from the Christian communities known to have existed in the region of Hadrian's Wall. At the Catstane cemetery, Kirkliston, Midlothian, a Christian cemetery has been excavated with burials laid out in 'long cists' – graves made with stone slabs. These long-cist cemeteries are among the earliest pieces of evidence for Christianity in Celtic lands, and they are found in southern Pictland, particularly in Fife, as well as the Lothians. There is no date for the Fife cemeteries, but the Catstane cemetery, as well as having a memorial stone with Latin lettering datable to the late fifth or early sixth century, has provided radio-carbon dates that suggest the cemetery was in use by the early fifth century AD.

It is unlikely, as Dr Kathleen Hughes stressed, that either Ninian's or Columba's mission had any immediate far-reaching effect on the religious beliefs of the Picts. Dr Hughes suggested that in fact Christianity did not become well established in Pictland until the time of Nechton and the adoption of advice from Northumbria on such matters as the method of calculating the date of Easter in the early eighth century. She suggested that all Class I Pictish symbol stones (i.e. those comprising undressed stones with incised symbols only on them; see p. 100) belonged to a period of paganism, and that the appearance of Class II stones in the eighth century coincided with the spread of Christianity. In Adomnan's time, there were offshoot foundations from Iona in Pictland. Adomnan recorded that, in his own lifetime, the world had been twice ravaged by plagues. He said that Picts and Irish on both occasions escaped, owing to the importance of St Columba, whose monasteries 'placed within the boundaries of both peoples, are down to the present time held in great honour by them both'. From this it can be inferred that, by the seventh century, Christianity had spread in some measure among the Picts, not merely in the extreme South.

Archaeological evidence for early Christianity is extremely difficult to date, since Christian burials are always devoid of datable grave goods, and few churches were splendid enough to boast sculptures or inscriptions that can be dated.

In the Celtic areas, the earliest Christian cemeteries enclosed the burials with a circular 'vallum' or rampart (though the earliest cemeteries were unenclosed), which separated the sacred from the profane – the dead from the living. Such circular cemeteries are widespread in Pictland, but how early (or how recent) any of them is is impossible to judge. In some cases the churchyards have a medieval church built on

Figure 15 Hallowhill, Fife. Long-cist ceremony after excavation. Such long stone burial cists are typical of the earliest Christian cemeteries in Celtic Britain. There is a concentration of them in Fife and Angus. (Photo: David Longley)

top of the mound of what appears to be an Early Christian predecessor. On Irish evidence, before the Viking Age, churches and chapels would have been built of timber, and no early timber chapels have yet been excavated in Pictland, though one, probably of the Viking Age, was excavated at the Brough of Deerness, Orkney. The earliest churches in stone may date from the ninth century, but their simple plans are deceptive, and the foundations of unicameral (one-cell) buildings located within circular grave enclosures in Pictland could as easily belong to the twelfth century as the ninth or tenth. There were perhaps a few exceptions for, following Nechton's welcome to Northumbian masons, some churches in Anglo-Saxon style seem to have been built in Pictland. Despite claims, none has survived.

The finest of the supposed early churches in Pictland is that associated with the later monastery at Restenneth, Angus. Beneath a later medieval spire stands a tower (presumably originally attached to a timber nave) with typically late-Saxon-style pointed arch windows and a Saxon-style door. A case has been advanced for an early date, associating the tower with Nechton. According to this view, the lower part of the tower was the 'porticus' of a church built around 710, which was raised into a tower around 1100. Architecturally, however, there is no reason to date even the lower portion until after the amalgamation of the Picts and Scots, perhaps in the late eleventh century.

Figure 16 Remains of a vallum, Papil, Burra, Shetland. The modern churchyard wall is built on top of the vallum of the early Christian monastery. The present church is also built on the platform of an earlier predecessor. Papil has produced two notable early Christian sculptures (see Figures 97 and 100). (Photo: L.. Laing)

Figure 17 Restenneth Priory church, Angus. The present church is part of a medieval monastery and claims have been made that the tower dates back in part to Pictish times. Despite the Anglo-Saxon character of some features, however, it seems unlikely to predate the eleventh or twelfth centuries. (Photo: L. Laing)

Of similar date is the chapel and tower of St Regulus (or St Rule) in St Andrews, which probably dates from the early twelfth century. This has a slightly wider chancel to the east. Again its windows are survivors of late Anglo-Saxon style.

Of the other surviving stone structures put up by the Church in what had been Pictland, mention may be made of two Irish-style round towers, one free-standing at Abernethy, Perthshire, the other now attached to the later Brechin Cathedral in Angus. As with their Irish counterparts, these towers have doors above ground level, originally reached by wooden stairs, and windows facing in other directions. The door at Abernethy is again in keeping with Anglo-Saxon masonry styles. The tower at Brechin has a fine ornamental doorway crowned with a Crucifixion, with flanking figures of hooded clerics on the jambs and crouching animals beneath. Both date from around the beginning of the twelfth century.

Of the great early Christian monasteries of Pictland, few visible remains survive. In Wester Ross, the monastery of Applecross was founded in c. 673 by St Maelrubha from Bangor in Ireland. Nothing now survives except for a cross-slab and traces of the vallum of the monastery. The valla of other lesser monasteries are visible on a number of sites, such as Papil on West Burra, Shetland, where the vallum is now under the churchyard wall.

Historically, relatively little is known about the Pictish Church in the time of Nechton and later. It has been suggested that he may have founded a bishopric at Abernethy, but this is not proven. In 721 an 'episcopus Scotiae Pictus' is recorded as attending a council in Rome, though whether his diocese was in Pictland or he was merely a Pict by birth is not clear.

Figure 18 Abernethy round tower, Perthshire. This is one of two surviving round towers of Irish style in Scotland and shows the influence of Scottic architecture. It probably dates from the later eleventh century, after the amalgamation of the Picts and Scots. A Class I symbol stone stands at the churchyard entrance. (Photo: L.. Laing)

The vast majority of evidence for the Church in Pictish lands takes the form of sculptures and the occasional item of metalwork (see Chapter 4). Apart from this there is a scatter of cross-marked stones without further elaboration that are assumed to have marked Pictish graves, as well as stones which seem to have come from composite slab-built shrines (of which the St Andrews shrine is the finest example; see p. 138), and possibly the evidence of Pictish square-enclosed graves.

The square-enclosed graves are a distinctive type of monument that has only relatively recently been recognized. These graves are found widespread in Pictish areas. North of the Mounth, burials seem to have been made under kerbed cairns, sometimes circular and sometimes rectangular. In the areas to the South, square and circular ditched barrows appear as crop marks and are the earthen equivalent of the northern cairns. These show some features that recall the Iron Age La Tène chariot (or rather cart) burials of eastern Yorkshire, and claims have been made that they are derived from them. This seems extremely unlikely since the Yorkshire burials represent a very local and restricted tradition. If an explanation for the rectangular form is needed, it is more likely to be found in the rectangular grave enclosures encountered on early Christian ecclesiastical sites elsewhere in the Celtic areas – there is a series in Ireland, particularly in County Kerry. But this cannot yet be proved, since it is not certain whether such Pictish burial mounds are pagan, Christian, or both.

One possibly ecclesiastical site has produced an array of artefacts. This is the cemetery and settlement on the tidal island of Birsay in Orkney. It was long assumed that Birsay was a monastery, but its ecclesiastical status in the Pictish period is in fact not known. There was a Norse cemetery and a substantial church on the site in the twelfth century, and this was preceded by a cemetery within a vallum, but current opinion dates the latter to the eleventh century

Figure 19 Round tower doorway, Brechin, Angus. The tower is now attached to Brechin Cathedral, but around 1100 was probably built freestanding. The ornate doorway is flanked by figures and animals, and surmounted by a crucifixion. (Photo: David Longley)

Figure 20 This fine arch is all that remains of what must have been a large church at Forteviot, Perthshire. Forteviot was one of the later capitals of Pictland and had a *palacium* (palace). The arch, made of a single stone, has two clerics on either side of what may be a lamb, but the precise meaning is obscure. Width: 2 m. (Photo: Royal Museums of Scotland)

Figure 21 General view of the tidal island of Birsay, Orkney. the main remains are of the twelfth-century church and adjacent bishop's palace, with Viking houses and the complexes known as Earl Sigurd's hall and Earl Thorfinn's palace. The restored Pictish stone is to the left of the church in the Pictish cemetery. (Photo: L. Laing)

Figure 22 Handbell, found near Birsay in a cist apparently intended for it. It was laid mouth upwards, covered by a stone. Such bells, usually without clappers, were characteristic of the Church in Celtic lands. The most famous example is that of St Patrick in Ireland. Height excluding handle: 30 cm. (Drawing: Anderson, 1881)

rather than earlier and sees it also as Norse. Given, however, the continuity of religious sites, it seems quite conceivable that Birsay had a Pictish monastic foundation. Further, the abundant evidence for metalworking and other activities on the site in the seventh and eighth centuries may have arisen from a secular community attached to the monastery, in the manner in which such lay communities were associated with Irish monasteries. The most interesting finds from Birsay comprise the remains of metalworking found in the vicinity of a well. This metalworking debris is considered later (see p. 72). A cross-marked stone and an iron handbell, the latter a residual in later Norse levels, might point to a Pictish monastic phase, though of course the bell could have been looted by the Norse from elsewhere. An iron slotted-topped implement and an enamelled bronze pin of Irish type hint at an an Irish connection.

Figure 23 Irish object from Birsay. A few such items suggest Irish connections. This slotted iron piece may have been used for weaving rush matting. Similar objects are known from Dunadd, Argyll and from Irish sites. Length: 14.6 cm. (Drawing: Amanda Straw)

CHAPTER 2

The Scots

The Scots were Irish who came across to Britain, first as allies of the Picts and raiders on the Roman province of Britannia, then as settlers. Although the archaeological evidence for Scottish raids and settlement is relatively sparse, there is, fortunately, more documentation on the history of the Irish settlers in western Scotland. This is because the Irish themselves recorded events in the colony, and, subsequent to the foundation of the Irish-derived monastery at Iona by St Columba in 563, records were kept there of events in the Scottish kingdom of Dalriada. Alongside this body of material there are supplementary sources of information, including the invaluable Life of St Columba set down not long after the saint's death by a later abbot of Iona, Adomnan. Less abundant is the knowledge derived from archaeology, although Dunadd in Argyll, usually taken to be the capital of the Dalriadic Scots, has been extensively excavated, and the information from this site can be supplemented from a few others of lesser significance. For the Columban foundation at Iona there is both archaeological and documentary evidence, as well as an important group of works of art.

Links Between Ireland and Scotland in Prehistory

Argyll is a rugged and untamed part of Britain – a land of mountains, lochs, bogs and rocky promontories, partly sheltered by a collection of islands, mostly inhospitable. Today the roads are narrow and winding, and the land supports little arable farming. In the first millennium AD it could hardly have seemed a jewel worthy of capture. Yet Argyll and the adjacent Inner Hebrides saw extensive colonization in earlier prehistory, and the landscape is marked with the burial mounds and mysterious cup-and-ring rock engravings of a flourishing Bronze Age culture.

The distance from Scotland to north-east Ireland is not great (the shortest sea route is less than twenty-five miles), so it would not be surprising if close contacts existed between the two areas in prehistoric and early historic times. Most of the evidence for the links with northern Ireland comes from the Solway–Clyde region, where finds have included, for example, Irish-style Neolithic pottery and axes.

Occasional bronzes of Irish origin point to continuing contacts between Argyll and northern Ireland in the earlier part of the Bronze Age, and in the later Bronze Age a concentration of goldwork finds in Argyll and Bute suggest renewed contact with Ireland.

By the early Iron Age there is more substantial evidence for links between Scotland and Ireland. It has to be said, however, that although the indication is of contacts between northern Ireland and western Scotland, there is no dense concentration of finds of objects of Irish type specifically in Argyll.

Archaeologists often depend on pottery for demonstrating cultural connections between areas, but unfortunately there is very little native pottery of the Iron Age and early medieval periods in Ireland, except for a category of very coarse vessels known as 'souterrain ware'. As the name suggests, this has been found in the underground passages or souterrains of north-eastern Ireland. There is reason to believe, however, that this type of pottery was not widely used before the early medieval period, and it is thus of little use in establishing contacts between the two areas before the traditional period of the settlement of Dalriada.

The artefacts found in Scotland and Ireland that do attest Iron Age contacts between the two areas are very varied. They are recognizable perhaps from the first century AD onwards, when the links with Ireland seem to be most strong in south-west Scotland and the Hebrides.

Particularly interesting is a shared art-style which involved creating patterns with compass arcs. This type of ornament was probably developed in eastern Ireland, where it is encountered on a series of pieces of bone found on a much earlier prehistoric chambered tomb site at Lough Crew, County Meath. The Lough Crew bone slips include pieces of what may have been combs, and a comb decorated with a compass-drawn design has been found in a lake-dwelling at Langbank, Ayrshire. The Langbank comb is a classic example of Celtic ambiguity: one way up the design is abstract, the other it takes on the form of a cartoon-like face.

'Crannogs' (dwellings in lakes) are a feature of Irish archaeology, so their appearance in western Scotland may be an indication of the contact between the two areas. Although the crannog at Oakbank, Perthshire, has radio-carbon dates centred on the sixth century BC, and there are a few other instances of crannogs which apparently date back to the sixth or fifth centuries BC, if not earlier, nearly all the Scottish crannogs seem to have been in use in the first or second centuries AD or later.

The Langbank comb might have been seen as an import, were it not for the fact that the style of art to which it belongs is encountered on other objects in both areas. The 'face' on the comb also bears certain similarities to faces that can be discerned in the ornament on a series of high-relief, modelled bronze plates of uncertain function found in Ireland. They are known after a classic example as 'Monasterevin discs'.

Figure 24 Crannog, Loch Scridain, Glen More, Mull. Crannogs – artificial islands made of layers of stones and brushwood – are a feature of Irish archaeology and occasionally occur in Scotland (and in one case in Wales). In Ireland they are high-status sites and mostly date from the early medieval period. Some in Argyll were used as late as the seventeenth century. (Photo: David Longley)

These discs have other elements in their design, including fine-lined trumpet patterns and snail-like bosses, which link them to a series of bronze armlets produced around the second century AD in what later became Pictland. One of these 'Caledonian' armlets as they are called, was found at Newry in County Down, reinforcing the link.

Other finds suggest a more warlike connection. Knobbed bronze spearbutts, which are known to have been made in Scotland, have been found as far afield as Bute and Tiree in the Hebrides and further north in Orkney. Similar spearbutts are a feature of the Irish Iron Age. The opposite flow of traffic includes a weaving comb and a pin from Ireland that must have been made in northern Scotland.

When this evidence is reviewed as a whole, it can be seen that it points to a network of high-level communication between the two areas which goes back at least as early as the first century AD.

The Scots in Ireland

In general terms the archaeology of north-east Ireland in the Iron Age is very different from that of Atlantic Scotland. The dominant type of settlement is an earthen ring-fort known as a 'rath', which comprises an earth bank with (usually) a single entrance enclosing a circular central area in which a farmstead was built. Most are fairly small, about 30 m in diameter, and some appear to have had the interior deliberately heightened. In areas that are very rocky, the raths are built with stone ramparts rather than earth and are known as 'cashels'. At Deer Park Farms, County Antrim, a waterlogged house was found inside a rath, with a double row of wicker walling, a central hearth, and bedding against the wall. In all, five wicker houses of the seventh to eighth

Figure 25 Monasterevin disc and Langbank comb. The bronze disc (top), from Monasterevin, Ireland, is of unknown function. It is decorated with characteristic high-relief modelling and elongated trumpet patterns. The similarity to a surprised face is echoed in a bone comb (bottom) from Langbank, Renfrewshire, from a crannog. The compass-drawn ornament of the Langbank comb betrays its connection with similar compass-decorated bonework from Ireland. Both probably belong to the early centuries AD. Disc diameter: 30.6 cm; comb width: 3.8cm. (Drawings: L. Laing)

Figure 26 Deer Park Farms, County Antrim. This rath, excavated between 1984 and 1987, was remarkable for preserving the waterlogged remains of several houses with wickerwork walls mostly of hazel, occupied between c. AD 600 and 1000. The houses, which were double-walled, had their walls pushed over when abandoned. Three or four houses with an internal diameter of 5–7 m were in use at any one time. About forty buildings were discovered on this site. (Photo: © Crown copyright. Reproduced with the permission of HMSO)

centuries AD were found at this site, and it appeared that the space between the inner and outer wall was filled with straw, moss and heather as a form of cavity wall insulation. Houses were sometimes round, sometimes rectangular, the change from round to rectangular perhaps being due to Roman or Anglo-Saxon influence, though there is no evidence for rectangular houses before the eighth or ninth century. It has been estimated that there are about forty thousand raths in Ireland.

In contrast, houses built in lochs (crannogs), are comparatively rare and were high-status sites, probably of chiefs or kings. They were usually circular, built on islands composed of alternate layers of stones and brushwood, with vertical timbers driven into the bed of the loch. Although some raths and crannogs may date back in some parts of Ireland to the later Bronze Age, the vast majority seem to have been in use between the fourth and ninth centuries AD.

There are a few 'promontory forts' in northern Ireland, of which one good example can be seen at Larrybane, County Antrim. Here the finds include an assortment of bone and stone implements, a fragment of a fine multi-coloured glass bangle and an assemblage of souterrain

Figure 27 At Coolcran, County Fermanagh, a souterrain comprising a passage 6.5 m long ending in a wood-lined pit, 9 × 3.5 m in extent, was discovered. Sawn oaks were used in the construction and provided a tree-ring date in the ninth century. Souterrains, which are found in both Ireland and Scotland, seem to have been the 'cellars' of above-ground huts. They were normally constructed of stone. (Photo: © Crown copyright. Reproduced with the permission of HMSO)

ware. The occupants, who seem to have burned peat on their fires, were both farmers and fishermen. Dating of the fort is difficult, but seems to have centred on the seventh or eighth century AD.

The souterrains are often found with raths, and like their Pictish counterparts (p. 76) were underground passages associated with above-ground buildings. A wood-lined souterrain is known at Coolcran, County Fermanagh, but most are constructed with a trench, lined with drystone walling or slabs. The roof could have projected above the ground, as in Pictland, and they were probably used for the storage of dairy produce. Souterrains are not known from the areas of the Dalriadic settlement of Scotland.

Changing Patterns in Celtic Britain and Ireland

During the first to third centuries AD the links between Scotland and Ireland were growing: social and economic changes were affecting both areas and new political configurations were being formed. These changes are reflected in the archaeological record of what became the territories of the Picts (see p. 75). These trends did not result in changes to the basic population, but in the emergence of new centres of power. This is perhaps seen most clearly in the transition from large forts (which accommodated groups of families) to smaller duns. Although duns clearly originated earlier, the concentration of Roman finds from them points to a main period of occupation centring on the second century AD.

The factors behind these changes are complex to understand, but include the constant awareness of Rome on the doorstep. The Roman Empire was both a threat and a promise: the threat lay in the possibility of Roman military advance and conquest, the promise in the material benefits the Roman world could bestow, either willingly or unwillingly. The threat probably led to the new alliances and a solidarity in the face of a shared enemy; the promise brought new wealth, either looted or acquired legitimately through trade or buy-offs.

In Ireland there may have been more of a threat from Rome than is often supposed. Apparently, Agricola contemplated an expedition to Ireland in the later first century AD, though he was never able to implement his plan. Partly with this objective in mind the outpost fort at Loudoun Hill in Ayrshire may have been built. In any event, where Roman soldiers did not go, merchants were not afraid to tread.

During the first and second centuries AD, the volume of trade with the Roman world was not particularly organized. A possible exception to this was a trading base which seems to have been established at Stoneyford on the Nore, where the cremation (in a glass vessel) of what has been taken to be the body of a Roman merchant was found in a native rath, associated with a bronze mirror and a glass 'tear bottle'. Trade, however, almost ceased in the third century AD, to revive dramatically in the fourth.

By this time, however, other factors were at work in the Irish economy and in Irish society. By the first century BC, and continuing into the first century AD, there seems to have been a general decline in farming. By around AD 225, however, the climate was improving again, and by the end of the third century AD there is evidence for recovery in many areas, including County Antrim. Some scholars have linked this recovery to the innovation in Ireland of farming methods derived from Roman Britain, most notably the use of the mould-board plough. Improved farming would have led to increased food supply, and this may be linked with possible evidence for a considerable population explosion in Ireland from AD 300 onwards, continuing perhaps into the fifth and sixth centuries. There is a notable dearth of Irish sites that can be dated confidently to the last centuries BC and first couple of centuries AD, but a plethora of sites apparently occupied between AD 300 and 700.

A population explosion would have had two results. The pressure on land would first have caused conflicts and feuds, and second would have made overseas ventures an exciting possibility. Both these things seem to have happened in Ireland. Warfare is reflected in Irish legends which may date back to around this period. These tell of petty feuds as well as the major conflict recorded in the epic saga cycle, the *Táin bó Cuailgne*. Such warfare, of course, is poorly reflected in the archaeological record, but archaeology can give some support to the legendary sources for Irish raids and settlement overseas.

Fable tells how Niall Noigiallach (Niall of the Nine Hostages) raided in the Hebrides, and recent historical research puts his activities in the 420s or 430s. He must be seen not as the first raider, but simply as the first historically documented Irish raider of Britain.

Fourth-century hoards of silverwork derived from Roman Britain have been found at Balline, County Waterford, and Coleraine, County Londonderry. Both finds contained silver ingots of a type used in the late fourth century as 'donatives' ('special' payments to soldiers and others). In the case of the Coleraine hoard, the ingots were associated with 1,506 Roman silver coins, as well as other pieces of silverwork. The ingots in the hoard may have reached Ireland not as loot but as payments, either to Irish mercenaries or as pay-offs to deter Irish raiders.

Roman Defences against Irish Raids

The first evidence available of Irish raids on western Britain is largely circumstantial, and comprises hoards of coins deposited in Wales in the late third and early fourth centuries AD. The first group of these coin hoards consists of issues of Carausius and Allectus, usurpers who formed a breakaway 'Empire' in Britain. Their rule came to an end in AD 296 when the legitimate emperor, Constantius Chlorus, came to Britain and defeated Allectus. Almost half of the hoards of Carausius and Allectus found in Britain have been recovered in Wales. If these are taken along with those of the preceding period (from AD 253), the distribution can be seen as predominantly coastal and western, pointing to general unrest and insecurity. This could most readily, though not necessarily, be explained by a threat from Ireland.

A second phase of hoarding, probably with a similar cause, can be seen in Wales in the time of Constantine the Great in the early fourth century.

The hoards themselves do not amount to proof of Irish activity, but additionally there is evidence for Roman military activity in the West. Around the turn of the third century, rebuilding took place at Chester which had been the Roman military base for North Wales, and a new fort was built at Lancaster. To this period too can probably be ascribed the building of a fort at Caer Gybi on Holyhead and another at Cardiff. The fort at Caer Gybi has a number of building features that are shared by a small fort south of the main one at Caernarvon. It has been

Figure 28 These items came from a hoard of Roman silverwork from Balline, northern Ireland. This and the Coleraine hoard contained stamped ingots of a type distributed in the late Roman Empire as donatives to troops and others. While the Balline hoard could have been loot, it could as easily have been a Roman buy-off. (Photo: National Museum, Dublin)

Figure 29 Entrance to the fort at Caer Gybi, Holyhead, Anglesey. This small Roman fort now forms the churchyard of St Gybi's church, as the site was supposedly given to him in the sixth century. The fort was built in the fourth century, along with the Lower Fort at Caernarvon, probably as part of a defence against Irish raiders. (Photo: L. Laing)

suggested that all these sites were linked with the fortified towns of Caerwent and Carmarthen in south Wales as part of a defensive scheme put in hand by Constantius Chlorus at the end of the third century AD. Signal stations to give advance warning of raids may have been built at Loughor and Pembroke in south Wales, and there is evidence for a fleet based on the Bristol Channel in the form of an inscription found at Lydney, Gloucestershire, mentioning a 'prefect in charge of the fleet's supply depot'.

The Colonization of Dalriada

Possibly because of the success of Roman defences, long-term Irish settlement in Britain eventually took place in Scotland, beyond the areas under Roman control. The earliest tradition concerning the Irish settlement of western Scotland comes from a tenth-century copy of a seventh-century document known as the Senchus fer nAlban (Tradition of the Men of Scotland). The Senchus is a kind of early Domesday Book, listing holdings in Argyll and also providing a muster of land and sea forces. It is concerned with lineages (the Irish word is *cenel*, perhaps best translated as 'people'). The Senchus shows that the colonization was spearheaded by Fergus, son of Erc, the descendant of Nes (possibly a river goddess), who came with his brothers and established control before dying in 501. It would seem that Fergus' main arena of activity was Kintyre. The Senchus also records that Fergus' brothers, Loarn and Oengus, established themselves in Lorn (where the lineage became the Cenel Loairn) and Islay (where the line was that of the Cenel nOengusa). This all seems too neat an explanation for the origins of the three divisions of Dalriada. Modern opinion favours the view that the 'sons' of Fergus were invented to account for an earlier migration to Argyll from Ireland, where Cenel nOengusa was already established before Fergus' time.

A separate origin legend from Ireland suggests that a certain Cairpre Riata led a much earlier colonization in Scotland – the Irish source puts it at ten generations before the time of Fergus. By interpreting this strictly with twenty-five years to a generation, a date in the third century AD or even earlier is given. This seems impossibly early, but might explain the fourth-century alliance between Picts and Scots. Some confirmation of the story is provided by Bede who believed that Argyll was colonized by a certain Reuda, presumably the same person as Cairpre Riata.

In any event, Fergus appears to have been succeeded first by his son (who died c. 507), then his two grandsons, Comgall (who died c. 537/8) and then Gabran (who died c. 558). Comgall's line gave his name to the modern district of Cowal where they ruled and apparently, in the eighth century, ousted the Cenel nGabrain which in earlier times had also been dominant in Kintyre. By this time Arran had probably also come under the control of the Dalriadic kings.

There is no reason to suppose that the early colonization of Scottic Dalriada was other than fairly peaceful. Nor is there evidence that the territories of Irish Dalriada were not under the control of Fergus and his descendants for some time after the migration to Scotland. Indeed, at Druim Cett (Daisy Hill, near Limavady, County Derry) a convention was held in 575 in the presence of St Columba to discuss the relationship of Irish Dalriada to the then King of Scottish Dalriada, Aedan mac Gabrain, and to the northern Ui Neill's leader, Aed, son of Ainmire. The outcome of the convention was the decision that the right to the armed forces of Irish Dalriada should go to Aed, as overlord of northern Ireland, but that Aedan was to continue to rule over the Irish territories, and to extract taxes and tributes.

In Ireland, the neighbours of the Dalriadans were the Ulaid (on the coast of County Down) and the Dal nAraide (or Cruithne), who seem to have been related in people's minds with the Picts. The Irish Dalriada were in conflict with the Ulaid, but certainly as early as the beginning of the seventh century, and probably much earlier, good relations had been established with the Dal nAraide: Aed Dub mac Suibne, their king at the end of the sixth century, spent some time in Scottish Dalriada as a cleric. However, the Ulster Dalriada came into conflict in the early seventh century with their neighbours. A battle at

Figure 30 (overleaf) Ireland and Dalriada. Scale is in miles

Figure 31 (overleaf) Area of Irish settlement in Scotland. Dots are place-names of Irish derivation. Scale is in miles

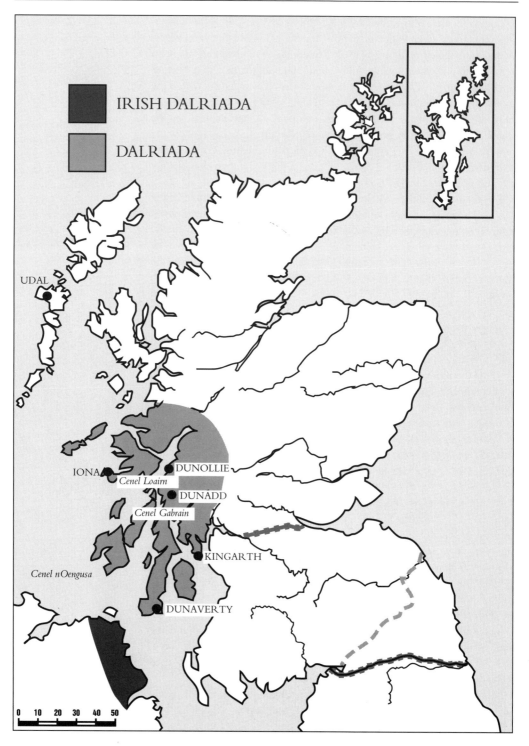

IRISH DALRIADA

DALRIADA

UDAL

IONA
Cenel Loairn
DUNOLLIE
DUNADD
Cenel Gabrain

Cenel nOengusa

KINGARTH

DUNAVERTY

0 10 20 30 40 50

Figure 30

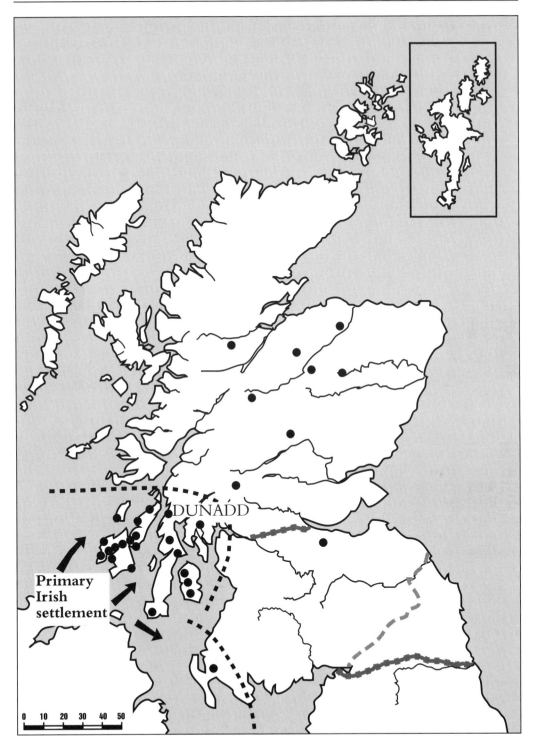

Primary
Irish
settlement

DUNADD

0 10 20 30 40 50

Figure 31

Mag Rath, fought in 637, resulted in the defeat of the Scottish Dalriadic king, Domnall Brecc, whose track record in other arenas of war was one of repeated defeat. After Mag Rath, another dynasty was established as rulers over Irish Dalriada, and the Scottish kingdom continued alone.

The early history of the Scottish kingdom of Dalriada is scrappy and confusing, and mostly comprises lists of names and sieges. The main sources are primarily annals, records of sequences of occurrences. It is notable that the early entries in the Anglo-Saxon Chronicle (which was partly inspired by the Irish Annals) took place in leap years! The idea of annals is a classical one, developed by Eusebius of Caesarea in the early fourth century, when he attempted to synchronize Roman history with earlier traditions about Greece, the Near East and the Old Testament. The outcome was a World History to which later writers added.

In Ireland, monks attempted to graft events from their own, initially pagan, past on to the Eusebian and later World Chronicle. The original versions incorporated references to European events which can be independently dated, but many of these disappeared in later transcripts, leaving only native, independently undatable events. Unfortunately for students, the AD system of dating, first worked out systematically for Britain by Bede, was not employed for the annals, and dates were added according to different systems by later copyists and annotators from the fourteenth century onwards. The resultant confusion caused some copyists to repeat the same event at different points in the sequence, and it has to be said that there are no truly 'historical' dates in the Irish Annals before the end of the seventh century at the earliest.

The Irish Annals that survive are all versions of earlier texts, copied in the eleventh century and later. The three main collections are the Annals of Innisfallen, which have been very extensively edited in modern times, the Annals of Ulster and the Annals of Tigernach. All three have material in common. The Annals of Innisfallen seem to have been set out in part at the end of the eleventh century, while Tigernach and Ulster belong to the fourteenth and fifteeenth centuries. Both seem to owe a debt to a common lost source, sometimes called the Ulster Chronicle, which may have been set down on Iona, though later entries in the Annals of Ulster appear to have been set down at Bangor in Ireland.

The history of Dalriada prior to the time of Columba is sketchy to say the least. There is a hint that Christianity was well established by the time of Domangart, son of Fergus, for the latter appears to have died as a cleric, as did his grandson, Aedan.

The first king to figure in events outside Dalriada was Gabran, who seems to have conducted expeditions to the east of his territory, as far afield as the Forth, where he may have been in conflict with Britons. In one source he is called 'king of the Forth'. Gabran may, however, have also campaigned in Pictland (it has been suggested that Gowrie in Strathtay is named after him), for in the year of his death (c. 558) a 'forced withdrawal' from the territory of the Pictish king, Bridei mac Maelcon, is documented.

In the reign of Gabran's successor, Conall, Columba left Ireland for Scotland. Columba stayed for a while with Conall, who is reputed to have given him Iona for his monastery, though Bede says he was given the island by the Picts. Columba found the monarchy in Dalriada not fully stablized, and it is probable that his influence was a factor in the strengthening of Dalriada. In 568, Conall appears to have joined forces with the King of Meath in an expedition to the Western Isles. It is likely his reign ended in civil disturbances between rival factions in Dalriada, one outcome of which may have been his death in 574.

Conall's successors were two of his cousins, Eoganan and Aedan. Aedan mac Gabran emerges from the dry entries of the Annals as a dynamic and forceful leader, who established his overlordship over the other families of Dalriada. Columba preferred Eoganan as the choice for king, but was chastized by an angel for his choice. Columba's role in the selection of the king shows his extraordinary power in politics. It was in Aedan's time that the Conference of Druim Cett took place.

There are many stories about Aedan's activities round the Forth, which may in part be true, and more about his activities in Pictland, including his expedition to the Orkneys in 581, whose (Pictish) king had earlier submitted to Bridei and sent hostages. Aedan is also reported as having joined forces with the Ulaid from northern Ireland to help the Britons against the Northumbrians at Bamburgh, and he also appears to have sent help to the British against the English at Degsastan in 603, where the English were victorious. After this time, it was said, 'no king of the Scots ever dared to meet the English in the field'.

After an intervening reign of which virtually nothing is known, the kingship of Dalriada passed to the warlike but singularly unsuccessful Domnall Brecc. Domnall held a notable reputation as a warrior, and his early years may have seen him successful in southern Pictish territory. A reprisal came in 636 when he was defeated within his own lands. He involved himself in support of an exile at Mag Rath in Ulster in 637 (thus alienating Iona, where Columba had said the Dalriadic kings should never wage war on the kin of the saint). Domnall died in Strathcarron at the hands of Owen (a king of the Britons of southern Scotland) in 643: 'I saw an array, they came from Kintyre, and splendidly they bore themselves around the conflagration . . . I saw great sturdy men, they came with dawn. And ravens gnawed the head of Dyfnwal Frych [Domnall Brecc]', said a contemporary poet.

By the mid-seventh century the kingdom had split into tribal group-ings dominated by at least seven families, each of which may have had its own assemblies and law, its hereditary king (ri) and inauguration rites. One of these rulers was high king over the rest. He seems to have been drawn from the descendants of Comgall and Gabran.

Unity was restored to Dalriada under Ferchar 'the Tall', in *c*. 680–696, one of the Cenel Loairn. Although the kingship passed once again to the Cenel nGabrain, for the next two centuries the Picts held military power in northern Scotland. From *c.* 741 for a century, Dalriada was mostly under the control of Pictland, and its history was traced as part of the story of the Picts (p. 17). The situation prevailed until, in obscure circumstances, a Dalriadic king, Kenneth mac Alpin (whose father's name is Pictish), united Picts and Scots under a Gaelic-speaking monarchy in 843/4.

The Beginnings of Christianity in Ireland

The religious beliefs of the pagan Irish were in line with those of the rest of the pre-Christian Celts. Patrick was the most famous but not necessarily the first Christian in Ireland. It is quite possible that in the fourth century some Christians were among those who were trading and possibly even settling in Ireland. It is likely that these immigrants gave rise to a small but significant number of Christian converts in the east of Ireland, for it was to minister to a Christian community that Pope Celestine sent Bishop Palladius from Gaul in 431.

Among the captives carried off from Britain by Irish raiders was St Patrick. Fortunately an account of his early history exists in Patrick's Confession. He makes it clear that his parents were Romano-Britons of high status, living in Britain, probably, it has been inferred, in the region to the immediate south of Hadrian's Wall. Patrick's arena was in the north of Ireland, and his Confession suggests that when he was taken, at the age of sixteen, to serve six years of slavery in Ireland he may have been a pagan, but was converted during his slavery. This implies the presence in northern Ireland of other Christians. He eventually escaped and, after a period probably spent in Gaul, perhaps as a deacon at Auxerre, returned to Ireland from Britain to begin his ministry.

Despite the activities of Palladius and Patrick, Christianity was slow to take hold in Ireland, and had to fight a long tradition of Celtic paganism which was eventually modified and assimilated into Christian belief in acceptable guises. Pagan custom still survived in the inauguration of kings as late as the twelfth century, as the writings of Gerald of Wales show.

The Church in Britain and Europe was organized on diocesan lines. The essence of a diocesan structure, however, is its metropolitan sees, and there were no towns in Ireland. The earliest sees may have been based on old tribal centres.

Monasticism

Monasticism originated as a reaction to the highly civilized urban institution that was the Church in the Mediterranean in the fourth and fifth century. Christianity was a religion that combined a high philosophical content with elements of Eastern mystery cults, and was also to be equated with the Establishment. The urban Church was essentially a middle-class phenomenon. By this time it is therefore not altogether surprising that within the Church in the eastern Mediterranean there grew up a reaction which called for rejection of urban values and intellectualism, and for the abandonment of materialism and a return to basic spiritual values. Thus began monasticism. Asceticism appealed to peasants 'dropping out' and living solitary lives. The first was St Anthony (c. AD 269), and the movement gained particular momentum in the desert areas of Syria and Egypt, where the 'fathers' (apa, hence the word abbot) were seen as models for the ascetic life. Their sayings were essentially folk wisdom and, through appealing directly to the populace in words they could understand, ascetics acquired power in society and provided an acceptable 'escape valve' for possible insurgence. The earliest desert fathers were solitaries, though not all took their isolation to the lengths of Symeon Stylites on his column. Groups banded together to form monasteries, which initially were the ecclesiastical equivalents of Roman forts, built to a rectangular plan with high walls both to isolate the monks within them and to serve as a defence against desert marauders.

From the eastern Mediterranean, monasticism spread in the late fourth and early fifth century to Gaul, where St Martin founded institutions at Liguge (near Poitiers) and Marmoutier (near Tours). Near Marseilles, other monasteries were founded by John Cassian and Victor. At Lérins, Honoratus founded yet another monastery. It was probably from southern Gaul, Aquitaine and perhaps Spain that monasticism spread to Britain and Ireland at the end of the fifth century, though there is little evidence of its becoming established before the sixth.

It was long thought that remains uncovered at Tintagel in Cornwall belonged to a monastery founded in the later fifth century, but this view seems no longer tenable. It has now to be admitted that there is no good documentary evidence for monasteries in Britain or Ireland before the sixth century, or the very end of the fifth in the case of Wales.

The first monasteries in Britain and Ireland were not like the carefully laid out institutions of the later medieval orders. Indeed, the idea of monastic planning did not come to western Europe until Carolingian times (in the early ninth century). Before that, monasteries were haphazard collections of buildings, cemeteries and working areas within an enclosure. It was such a monastery that Columba founded at Iona.

Columba and Iona

The first Christian leaders in Ireland, such as St Patrick, were probably peripatetic, and the fifth- and sixth-century sees seem to have been based on tribal territories, with ecclesiastical centres established near existing tribal foci.

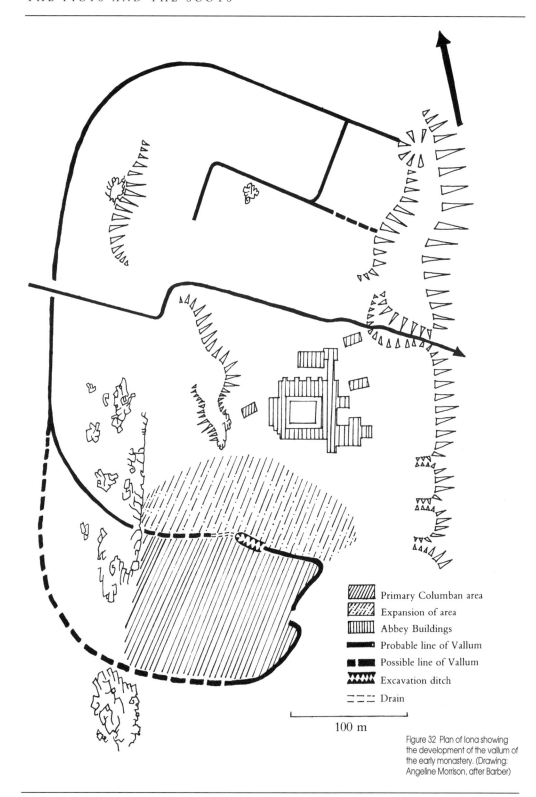

Primary Columban area
Expansion of area
Abbey Buildings
Probable line of Vallum
Possible line of Vallum
Excavation ditch
Drain

100 m

Figure 32 Plan of Iona showing
the development of the vallum of
the early monastery. (Drawing:
Angeline Morrison, after Barber)

The pattern of monasteries appears to have been grafted on to the existing network of regional, tribally based sees during the sixth century, and monasteries co-existed with regional churches in what seems to have been a fairly complex pattern of relationships. Monasticism grew in importance in the seventh and eighth centuries, but the Church in Ireland, as elsewhere in Celtic Britain, never became totally monastic as has sometimes been supposed.

One territorial confederacy of monasteries, however, emerged in the sixth century: the group of houses founded by Columba.

Columba is a key figure in any study of the Church in Celtic areas for, unlike many of the early Celtic saints, the Life of Columba was set down in writing by one of his successors as abbot of Iona, Adomnan. Though writing about a century after the saint's death in 597, Adomnan had access to material written shortly after Columba died and was able to speak to old men who had known Columba in their early youth. Accordingly, although there is much in the Life which is totally legendary such as accounts of routine miracles that did not happen, there is also a body of information that is almost certainly factual.

Almost nothing is known about Columba's early life. He was born in County Donegal, possibly at Gartan, *c.* 521. He was the grandson of Conall Gulban, founder of one of the branches of the Northern Ui Neill, the dominant dynasty in the northern part of Ireland. His great-grandfather appears to have been none other than Niall of the Nine Hostages. His foster father was Cruithnechan. Two other figures are mentioned in his early life: the 'aged Gemman' under whom he studied, and Finian, who was probably bishop of Clonard in Leinster where the best collections of books in Ireland were to be found.

The circumstances of Columba's departure from Ireland are surrounded by mystery. There is no evidence that he had been an active religious figure in the period prior to his departure from Ireland, and Adomnan cryptically recounted that Columba was excommunicated by a synod on a charge of trivial and pardonable offences, for which he was subsequently pardoned. This would seem to be glossing over something more serious, for excommunication was not a punishment meted out lightly. The excommunication was lifted by a synod at Teltown, County Meath, of the Ui Neill high kings, and the pardon was only achieved after a struggle. It may well have been, as Dr A.P. Smyth has suggested, that the pardon was linked to a period of exile as a penance, for immediately afterwards Columba left for Dalriada with twelve followers.

Columba's offence can only be guessed at, but it may have been for his part in the Battle of Cul Drebene in 561. Certainly Columba (the 'dove') was not as gentle a figure as Adomnan and other later commentators liked to make out, and it may be that the scar he bore on his body, supposedly inflicted by an angel with a glass book, had been sustained in battle and had to be explained in other terms later. Columba was reputedly able to predict the outcome of battles, and relics of the

Figure 33 Aerial view of the vallum or enclosing bank of the Columban monastery, Iona. (Photo: RCAHMS)

saint seem to have been particularly potent on the battlefield – as late as 1314, a lost relic of the saint was carried before the victorious Scottish army in the Monymusk Reliquary (see p. 148) at the Battle of Bannockburn.

On reaching Scotland, Columba's first foundation may have been on Hinba, a site that cannot now be identified but may have been Jura. Later tradition claimed he founded Iona as soon as he arrived in 563, but the first Iona monastery could have appeared as much as ten years later. Apart from Hinba and Iona, Columba appears to have founded other monasteries in Scotland, for example Mag Luinge on Tiree, an island where monasteries were also founded by other Irish saints, Brendan and Comgall, both of whom visited Columba on Hinba.

Eileach an Naoimh (see p. 55) may have been a foundation of Brendan's.

Traditionally, Columba has been seen as the missionary who converted the Picts, and Bede stated expressly that his purpose in coming to Scotland was just this. This seems implausible, and it is also unlikely that his visits to Pictland were many in number. Adomnan described how Columba visited King Bridei of the Picts (probably at Craig Phadrig, Inverness) where Columba entered the stronghold by miraculously breaking the locks, and where the Pictish king hid behind his druid, Broichan. His objective was, said Adomnan, to gain safe conduct for his friend Cormac, who was going to visit the Orkneys which came under Pictish rule. At no time did he say that Columba converted Bridei, although he mentions the conversions of individual Picts. However it is generally assumed that, although Columba may not have carried out a major missionary campaign himself, Bede is unlikely to have invented the conversion from Iona of northern Picts, and certainly Iona was of great importance to the monasteries of Pictland in later times. Adomnan reported that Columban monasteries existed in Pictland in his time (i.e. the late seventh century).

During his career, Columba founded the monastery at Durrow, County Offaly, and other foundations started by Columba in Ireland are known. Later tradition ascribes a number of monasteries to him, but these were possibly daughter houses of Iona founded after his death.

Columba died on Iona on 9 June 597, and was succeeded by his assistant, Baithene, a member of his own family. During the seventh century, Iona played a major role in the conversion of the Anglo-Saxons. Oswald, the son of Aethelfrith of Northumbria, took refuge on Iona after his defeat by Edwin c. 616/17 (perhaps at Heavensfield), later returning to become King of Northumbria after Edwin died. Oswald asked Iona for a bishop to carry on the work of conversion in Northumbria, and Aedan was sent, establishing a monastery on Lindisfarne. Although he trained Anglo-Saxon monks, his successors Finan and Colman were both former monks from Iona. From Lindisfarne, the teachings of Iona were spread with the foundation of daughter houses at Melrose, Tynemouth, Hartlepool, Coldingham, Whitby and Lastingham.

The synod of Whitby in 664 brought an end to the Iona tradition of Christianity in Northumbria, but the influence of Iona remained there, albeit reduced, in the seventh century. King Aldfrith spent some time on Iona, where Irish sources relate he was a pupil of Adomnan. Adomnan himself visited Northumbria, and stayed at Monkwearmouth and Jarrow. From Adomnan's time, Iona was a major centre of learning, and here major annals recording events both in Ireland and in Scotland were set down. In the eighth century, Iona again became very influential in Ireland.

In 795 the monastery was plundered, and in 802 and 806 there were major Viking devastations – on the latter occasion, sixty-eight monks were killed. In 804, land for a new monastery was obtained at Kells and building began in 807. It was to this place that the Iona community was mostly transferred, and Kells became the main monastery of the Columban *paruchia* (parish).

The Early Monastery at Iona

The island of Iona is 5.5 km long and 2.5 km wide at its maximum, and is generally rocky with a jagged coastline. Although there is evidence for occupation in prehistory, there is none that at the time of the foundation of the Columban monastery the island was other than uninhabited. Most of the visible ecclesiastical remains on the island today belong to the twelfth-century and later Benedictine monastery, but these lie within the earthworks of the Dark Age foundation.

Adomnan referred to the vallum which served to define the early monastery's legal and spiritual boundary. The remains on the south part of the site are still impressive and complex, with two successive but overlapping periods of construction, comprising in each case a main enclosure with a south-westerly annexe. The full extent of the area within the earthworks seems to have amounted to eight hectares, making it similar in extent to such major Irish foundations as Clonmacnois, County Offaly, and considerably larger than other known Scottish early Christian monasteries.

The inner of the two main banks was substantial – excavation in 1956 showed it to have been about 4.5 m wide, and still to be standing to a height of 1.5 m. The rampart was built on a foundation of turf and had a flanking ditch cut out of solid rock to a width of 4.2 m. Other excavations showed the ditch to have been about 3 m deep. The picture that emerges is of a major constructional undertaking, hardly compatible with the efforts of the few followers of Columba, and implying a large community from an early stage in the monastery's history. Radio-carbon dates from two ditch sections dug in 1979 suggested that the earliest earthwork was constructed in the sixth century, to be replaced by a larger and more ambitious work in the early seventh century.

Adomnan said that Columba's monastery buildings comprised a church with attached chamber, a number of working and sleeping huts, a hut for himself where he had 'for his couch the bare rock, and for his pillow a stone', another hut in which Columba wrote, 'built in a higher place', a guest house, and a communal building, constructed in part round an open space. There were also outlying buildings including barns and a shed. Adomnan referred to oak being brought across from the mainland for building in his own time, and to wattle being used to build the guest house in Columba's time. He also talked of graves, including Columba's, which came to be marked by the stone he had used as a pillow. Of the buildings mentioned by Adomnan little trace has come to light in excavation, but a complex of postholes was found in 1967, cut down into natural sand to varying depths. These were interpreted as the remains of a round-ended building plus an alignment of postholes (perhaps a fence) extending to about 10 m.

In another area, in 1959, traces of a substantial building of continuous, vertically set planks was discovered, reminiscent of building work in the Anglo-Saxon royal palace site at Yeavering, Northumberland. Elsewhere there were indications of other timber buildings, and 'industrial' areas where iron and bronzework were carried out, as well as woodwork and perhaps leatherwork.

Excavations presently in progress are bringing to light more evidence for the early monastery at Iona. The new discovery came to light beneath the floor of St Ronan's church (which dates from the thirteenth century). It was found that two of the walls of the medieval church were built on top of a chapel, with walls bonded by clay. This perhaps dates from the latter part of the early Christian period (stone was not used in building before the eighth century). The excavators also found an earlier cemetery beneath the chapel which appears to belong to the early Christian monastery. One skeleton at least has been provisionally identified as female, perhaps pointing to a lay community attached to the monastery.

Pottery in the monastery appears to have comprised both locally made coarse vessels and imports. The latter included: souterrain ware from Ireland; the rim of a red-slipped vessel from North Africa, of the sixth century; some so-called 'E Ware', perhaps from the region around Bordeaux; and some pottery from North Germany or the Baltic, perhaps introduced at the time of the Vikings. The wide sources of the pottery imply the prosperous trading connections of the Columban monastery. Apart from the African piece, none of the pottery need have been in use on Iona before the eighth century. It might seem that instead the Columban monks used turned wooden vessels, of which three have been found, preserved in waterlogged conditions. The same deposit yielded a variety of prepared timbers, a bucket stave, spatulas, worn-out shoes, pieces of leather and a draw-string purse.

Among the small finds from the early monastery were: a flat-backed bronze head in somewhat Pictish style, 27 mm high, perhaps of the sixth century; a bronze bell and clay moulds for making domed glass studs, decorated with interlaced circles into which metal could have been set; a little crucible for casting metal or enamel; and a glass rod, decorated with a spiral trail, perhaps used for making beads or inlays, similar to several from Irish sites.

Of exceptional interest is the site known as Torr an Aba, which has traditionally been believed to be St Columba's cell in the Middle Ages. Although, of course, excavation was unable to prove or disprove this, examination of the site showed that a sub-rectangular building had been erected on the partly widened summit of a low knoll. This was constructed with turf or stone footings with thin stakes to make a

Figure 34 Bronze casting of a head in Celtic style, found at Iona. This was probably intended for a crozier or a shrine. It may date from the eighth century and is likely to have been made in the monastery. Height: 2.7 cm. (Drawing: Amanda Straw)

windbreak, perhaps with a wigwam-type of roof. Inside the hut the rock was carefully worked to make a bench, and dressed rocks were positioned to form three sides of a rectangle, which would have served as a level base for a wooden table top. The hut was subsequently abandoned, after perhaps being burned, but subsequently the site was levelled, with a pebble surface and a base set up to take a cross.

When the monks arrived, oak and ash were growing in the vicinity of the site they chose for their foundation. These were cleared away and cereals were grown, as well as holly which may have been needed in the production of ink. Animal bones show that the monks dined well on beef, mutton, venison, pork, seal and fish.

Alongside this archaeological evidence may be set information provided by Adomnan about the lifestyle of the monks. As in later monasteries, time was divided between devotional activities and everyday jobs. A senior monk acted as a dispenser of tasks, which included the collection of wood for buildings, the cultivation of the monastery's fields, the tending of the flocks of sheep and cattle, and the slaughter of animals for meat. Cattle were kept for milk, as well as meat, which was sometimes brought by pack-horse from the grazing ground.

Visitors to the island sometimes came by ferry from Mull, shouting for transport from the opposite shore. Some came from farther afield, and Adomnan described both skin boats, like the modern Irish curraghs, and timber-built vessels. Some of the skin boats had sails and oars. Adomnan said that apart from prayer Columba's main activities were study and writing. He was believed to have been the scribe responsible for the now-fragmentary psalter known as the Cathach of St Columba, which may date from his time or very slightly later and which is the oldest surviving Irish manuscript. Scholars are agreed that it was written either at Iona or at Derry. Clearly, too, there were workshops responsible for the carving of stone monuments. The earliest include a seventh-century inscription commemorating one Echoid, which was the name of one of Columba's followers and also of one of the early Dalriadic kings. The finest monuments (see p. 149) date from the eighth and ninth centuries.

Iona and the Vikings

Iona suffered serious attacks from the Vikings and the community transferred to Kells in the early ninth century, leaving only a few monks to maintain the community until the twelfth century when the Benedictine monastery was built.

Excavations have produced evidence for ninth-century burning, and the finds from Iona include a a cross with a Norse runic inscription (runes were a form of writing developed in Scandinavia). In the last years of the tenth century a Viking raid left a hoard of 350 Anglo-Saxon

Figure 35 This mount was probably part of a set of harness decorations of the late eight or ninth century, but has been converted into a brooch by a Viking owner. The design in the centre is a ubiquitous pattern that can be found in the west of Scotland and could have come from Iona. (Photo: Royal Museums of Scotland)

silver pennies, including a few struck by the Viking kings of York. They were buried somewhere in the vicinity of the abbey. Along with the coins were a bent silver bar, a gold loop, and a decorative silver and gold mount, probably of Anglo-Saxon workmanship.

Other Ecclesiastical Centres

Although Iona was pre-eminent as the major ecclesiastical centre of Dalriada, there were other foundations in western Scotland that provide an insight into the early Christian Church. The monastery of St Blane's at Kingarth in Bute is a good example. The surviving church (restored in the late nineteenth century) is of later medieval work, but occupies an earlier site. St Blane, who was a contemporary of Columba, is known from Irish sources to have been associated with this site, which might have been founded in the late sixth century.

The monastery at Kingarth is on two levels, the medieval church standing within a graveyard on high ground above a second graveyard on a lower terrace. The whole complex was enclosed by a stone-built wall, the equivalent of a vallum, which was just over 1 m wide and still stands to a height of just under 1 m, enclosing an area of one hectare. Below the churchyard, but still inside the vallum, are stone-built cells which may belong to the eleventh century. The stone buildings may have replaced earlier timber ones.

Although there have been no recent excavations, clearance in 1896 brought to light a variety of sculptures. These vary in date from the ninth and tenth centuries onwards. A series of pieces of slate with inscriptions in Irish lettering and with various designs incised on them were also found. Such 'motif-pieces' are particularly common on Irish sites, and a comparable series was found in the 'schoolroom' of the monastery at Nendrum, County Down. The excavations also produced evidence of industrial activity.

A major monastery dedicated to St Moluag was situated at Lismore in Lorn, but little of the site is visible today. A monastery on Eigg was burned in 617, probably by pagan Picts.

The ideal image of the early Christian Celtic saint must be a humble monk living on a remote storm-swept island or rock-stack. Tiny

Figure 36 Motif-pieces or 'trial-pieces', typical of a series found in the monastery of Kingarth, Bute. It is believed that these were practice designs that were later used in manuscipts or metalwork. The Kingarth series is the only collection of its kind in Britain, though similar assemblages are fairly common in Ireland. They date from the eighth to ninth centuries. (Drawing: Tasha Guest)

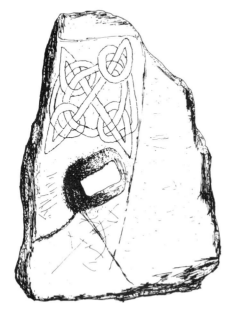

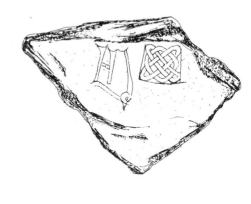

Figure 37 Hermit cells. These beehive monks' cells, which employ a distinctive type of corbelling, have probably survived due to the remoteness of the monastery on Eileach an Naoimh, a Hebridean island. Similar cells are known in Ireland, the most famous example being that on Skellig Michael off the coast of Kerry. They are difficult to date and could lie anywhere between AD 800 and 1200. (Photo: Scottish Development Department)

monasteries and hermitages of the early saints are to be found in remote situations, and few are more romantic than that at Eileach an Naoimh in the Garvellochs, off Islay. The site has never been excavated, but the remains comprise a series of drystone beehive cells in a small monastery, with a graveyard that has a special burial, known as 'Eithne's Grave'. Eithne was the mother of Columba, and the grave is set within a circular enclosure, about 5 m across, with two slabs marking the head of the grave and two the foot. One of these has a cross incised on it, perhaps of the seventh century. Whether or not the burial was that of Eithne, it is clear that here lay a highly revered person. The custom of marking a special grave with its own circular enclosure goes back to later prehistoric and Roman times in Britain, and recurs in the early Christian period. A similar site in Tiree can be seen at St Patrick's Chapel, Ciann a Mohoan, which has an enclosure wall with cells and hut platforms.

An idea of the development of the earliest church and cemetery sites of western Scotland can be formed by looking at St Ninian's Isle, Bute, a promontory on the west side of the island. Here the first Christian usage involved the formation of a cemetery with graves laid in long stone cists or boxes of slabs, a common device on Celtic burial sites of the early Middle Ages. Some of the burial sites, however, were found on excavation to be set at different angles, suggesting that, prior to its usage as a Christian burial place, it had been a pagan cemetery. The cemetery was next enclosed in a circular vallum made of stones and turf which excluded some of the burials. This circular planning of the churchyard is in contrast to the rectilinear planning of Iona (and, as far as we can judge, Kingarth), but in keeping with most early Christian Celtic cemeteries.

Probably there was an early timber chapel built within the cemetery at St Ninian's Isle. Nothing of it survives, and it was replaced by a stone chapel with a masonry altar, faced with slabs and containing a cavity for a relic (perhaps of St Blane) at the south end. This chapel may date from the early ninth century, perhaps from just before the time when the pagan Vikings harried the island.

Throughout the Inner Hebrides are scattered the grassed-over remains of early chapel sites. These are simple unicameral buildings which could date from any time between the eighth and fifteenth centuries. Large numbers can be seen on the island of Islay, where there are some fifteen such sites, many within oval enclosures. They are generally simple, drystone buildings, 4–6 m long and 3–3.5 m wide.

All over Dalriada can be found simple, cross-incised stones, attesting the strength of the Columban Church. No fewer than 31 can be found on Islay alone.

Figure 38 At Riskbuie, Colonsay, stood this face-cross. It is of a type found in Ireland (for example at Skellig Michael), but which is otherwise not represented in Britain. Dating from the seventh century, the design originated in the east Mediterranean. (Royal Museums of Scotland)

CHAPTER 3

Everyday Life of the Picts and the Scots

The Picts and the Scots were both Celtic peoples and as such shared much in common in their society and economy. Indeed, although there are certain types of artefact that seem distinctive to one or other group, much of the material equipment of both the Picts and the Scots was the same, and was generally similar to that of the other Celtic peoples of the early medieval period: the Irish, the Welsh and the Britons. In some measure, too, elements were shared in common with the Anglo-Saxons. An Anglo-Saxon knife, for example, is very similar to one used by an Irishman or a Pict of the same period. The same can be said of their settlements. This chapter begins by looking at the hierarchy of Celtic society, then discusses warfare and seamanship, trade, crafts and industries, leisure pursuits, and finally the homes of the Picts and Scots.

Celtic Society

Celtic society was, in the phrase coined by Prof. Binchy, 'tribal, rural, hierarchical and familiar (using this word in its oldest sense, to mean a society in which the family, not the individual, is the unit)'. It was a society that preserved the traditional structure of later prehistoric Europe, and as such provides us with a survival into the light of history of a part of our prehistoric past. In this society the status of women was much higher than in many others, with a complex social pyramid, at the top of which was a hierarchy of kings and at the bottom, slaves. Although comparatively little is known about the structure of society in Dalriada, one would not be far wrong in assuming that it was broadly comparable with that of Ireland, and the same, with certain strictures, may be said for Pictland.

In Ireland, the territorial unit was the *tuath* (tribe), a small area under the rule of a king. Kings themselves did not make laws; these were traditional and administered by professional jurists. A king's territory might extend to about a third of a modern county and would have about seven hundred fighting men within it. The king might be an overking, in that other kings had recognized his supremacy and may have sent hostages or paid him tribute. An overking, however, did not have jurisdiction over the people in the demesne of the underking, and would himself be similarly subject to a king of a province. It is clear that such a situation operated among the Picts since the king of the Orkneys sent hostages to the court of King Bridei in the time of Columba. The multi-regnal system seems to go back at least to the time of the Caledonians, for the Roman historian, Tacitus, wrote of many leaders (he called them *duces*), among whom one, Calgacus, was outstanding. In historical times the province to which Dalriada initially belonged was Ulaid, but it is clear that the various regions of Dalriada (Argyll proper, Knapdale, Kintyre and Cowal) came to be ruled over by the families of the two men Comgall and Gabran, grandsons of Fergus mac Erc.

Pictland was believed to be divided into seven regions (or kingdoms) which, although first documented fairly late in the early medieval period, seem to originate in more remote antiquity. For example the name of one of them, Fortriu (or Fortrenn), seems to be derived from the tribal name of the Verturiones mentioned in the fourth century. Each of these seven kingdoms was much larger than a *tuath*, and must have comprised something akin to the territory of an overking. Fortriu extended through Strathearn and Mentieth. Fib (Fife) is usually coupled with Fothriff, and collectively they comprised modern Fife and Kinross. The third region was Circhenn (or Circinn) which comprised Angus and the Mearns. The fourth area was Fotla (Atholl). North of the Dee lay the three kingdoms of Catt, Ce and Fidach. Catt (Caithness) does not figure in all accounts.

In general terms, kings inherited their kingdoms from their fathers, but Bede seems to have believed that the Picts were matrilineal. This has caused extensive debate, yet to be resolved. The documentary sources for Pictish matriliny are twofold. There is first a late Irish tradition that the Picts acquired womenfolk from the Irish on condition that Pictish kingship should pass through the female line. The second source is Bede, who also gave the story that the Picts were allowed to take wives from the Irish on condition that, when the succession was in doubt, the Picts should choose their kings from the female rather than the male line. Various attempts have been made to substantiate this but, as Dr A.P. Smyth has pointed out, Bede did not actually claim that succession was normally matrilinear, but only that it was employed in exceptional circumstances (a phenomenon found in other societies). Thus the legend could be seen as Irish propaganda that really related to Irish rights in the Pictish kingship and that Bede obtained his information from an Irish source. Smyth has argued that the names of the fathers of Pictish kings are given, which would be unlikely in a truly matrilinear society, and that the Picts took over from the Irish the formula *maqq* or *meqq* ('son of') in inscriptions. As things stand, the case for Pictish matriliny is not proven, and would not appear to be supported substantially by the evidence that survives, except in the very curious succession pattern.

In Dalriada also there was an unusual form of succession, known as 'tanistry'. This was patrilineal, but kings were often succeeded not by their sons but by their brothers and then their nephews. Direct patrilineal succession was also found.

Beneath the kings were the 'grades of nobility'. The nobility were the warriors, but they were also the patrons of the professional class which included the poets, artists, craftsmen, lawyers, historians and musicians. They were called in Ireland the *aes dana*, that is 'Men of Art', and their professional skill gave them status above that of their birth.

The chief social grade was of the ordinary freeman who was the farmer. This stalwart paid food-rent to the king. He may have been a client to a noble who lent him stock and offered him a certain degree of protection in return for work.

At the bottom of the social heap were the slaves. They are mentioned in the fifth century in Patrick's Letter to the Soldiers of Coroticus, from whom the Picts had been buying Christian slaves.

Above all, the kin group was the main unit of society. In Ireland this comprised the 'derbfhine', the descendants of a common great-grandfather, (i.e. everyone related to one another up to and including second cousins in the male line). The derbfhine owned property and was responsible for the liabilities of its members.

Warriors and Sailors

Warfare was one of the chief activities of the early Christian Celts. Something of the organization of warfare in Dalriada can be gleaned from the Senchus fer nAlban, a muster of warriors and sailors, which records how many men each household was required to put into the field. The Senchus refers to a *slogad* (or hosting) from each of the three peoples of Dalriada. The *slogad* was apparently one of three pledges that a king could demand of his people and, according to the Irish law code, the Crith Gablach, there were three kinds of such muster: to repel an invading army, to guard the border against invasion and to cross the border to deal with a rebellious tribe. The Senchus records that the Cenel nGabrain could muster three hundred men, the Cenel nOengusa five hundred and the Cenel Loairn six hundred, with a hundred others. The figures are probably on the low side, and other estimates from the available figures suggest that the Cenel nGabrain, which we are told had 430 houses, is more likely to have put eight hundred men in the field than three hundred, while the Cenel nOengusa probably mustered six hundred rather than five hundred. These figures tally quite closely with the seven hundred men each tribe was expected to

Figure 39 Representations of warriors and weapons on Pictish stones. These are from (a) Meigle No. 4, (b) Kirriemuir No. 2, (c) Saint Madoes, (d) Meigle No. 3, (e) Barflat, Rhymie, (f) Glamis No. 2, (g) Dull and (h) Inchbrayock. (Drawing: David Longley)

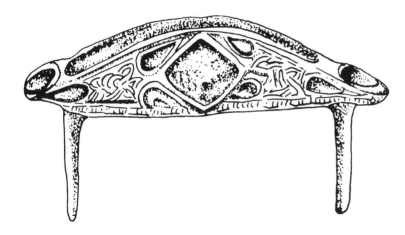

Figure 40 Bronze sword pommel decorated with double-strand interlace, late sixth or early seventh century. This was found at Culbin Sands, Moray. Although it shares some features in common with Anglo-Saxon and continental pommels, it is without precise parallel and is almost certainly Pictish. Width: 5.8 cm. (Drawing: Libby Cryer)

provide for its king in an Irish source. Irish sources speak of a military unit of 'thirty hundreds', which matches the three thousand men of a Roman legion. Within the army the basic unit was a hundred men, which was probably further subdivided.

Pictish warriors frequently appear on sculptures, and from this source a graphic picture can be formed of the Pictish army in action. The main weapons of the Pictish warrior seem to have been the spear and the sword. Spears are shown as having leaf-shaped blades and no butts. A leaf-shaped spearhead of this type is among the finds from Dunadd (see p. 70). Swords are shown with scabbards which were furnished with metal chapes, either expanded and crescentic, or moulded to the scabbard. A pair of what are probably scabbard chapes in silver were found in the St Ninian's Isle treasure. A fragmentary iron swordpoint with a pronounced midrib was among the finds from Dunadd. Sword pommels (an example of which was found in the St Ninian's Isle treasure) are of varying types, some similar to those fashionable in late Saxon England. A bronze pommel, decorated with interlace, was found at Culbin Sands, Moray, but is of a type not found represented on sculptures.

Battleaxes are sometimes wielded by sculpted warriors. Two figures seem to be using them on a stone from Glamis. They appear to be using axehammers, a type of axe of Roman derivation, also carried by the 'giant' on the Barflat, Rhynie stone. A T-shaped axe, not necessarily for use in battle, is found on the Aberlemno roadside slab. This type is found in late Saxon England and in northern Ireland.

Although Picts are shown carrying bows, there is no certain evidence for their use in battle, except possibly on the very late Sueno's stone from near Forres, Elgin. Crossbows (which originated in the Roman world) were used in hunting, and what may be a Pictish crossbow nut (used for catching the string and holding it back prior to release) has been found in Castle Urquhart, Inverness. Another (non-Pictish) crossbow nut of the Dark Ages has been found in a crannog at Buston, Ayrshire. Crossbows are depicted on the Drosten stone, St Vigeans, on the Shadwick stone, Ross and Cromarty, and on the Glenferness stone. Longbows appear on Sueno's stone.

Slings are not attested in sculpture. Some of the painted pebbles that have been found on broch sites may be slingshot, the painted designs being akin to the messages and designs sometimes put on Greek and Roman lead slingshot.

Armour has not survived from northern Scotland, though silver hooks in the Norrie's Law hoard may be from *lorica squamata*, a type of scale armour used by the Romans. The account of the original discovery mentions silver armour, and also a helmet and shield. Unless a small piece of beaten silver in the hoard came from a helmet constructed with plates on a frame, in the manner of Continental helmets, nothing survives of the helmet, but pieces of a large roundel of silver may have been the facing for a small, round composite shield.

In sculpture, however, there is plenty of evidence of Pictish armour. The best information comes from the Aberlemno churchyard cross, but if it is correct that the decoration on this represents combat between Picts and Anglo-Saxons, the figures on the right are Northumbrian warriors, not Picts. The Pictish warriors are carrying small round shields with pronounced, pointed bosses, and are apparently wearing stiff leather tunics. One of the dead, who may be an Anglo-Saxon, seems to be wearing chain mail. It is likely that both high-ranking Anglo-Saxons and Celts wore chain mail in battle, and pieces of mail have been recovered from Anglo-Saxon contexts. A helmet with a nose-guard appears on a slab from Benvie, and what appears to be a helmet with a vizor can be seen on a stone from Balblair. A Pictish symbol, often interpreted as a bow and arrow, on a stone from Congash may represent a helmet with crest and nose-guard.

Shields are of two types. The first is square or oblong, probably derived from the Roman *scutum*, but smaller and hand-held. An unusual type of notched shield appears on a stone from Ardchattan, Argyll, and on the St Andrews shrine. The second type, which is small and round, seems to have been the most popular and figures not only on stones but also in the Book of Kells. When not in use it appears to have been carried on a strap around the neck and must have been used in hand-to-hand combat.

According to Tacitus, the Caledonians used chariots at Mons Graupius. Chariots are probably the explanation for the heavy 'terrets' (rein guide-rings from the top of yokes) found in Caledonia in the early centuries AD. However, although chariots figure on Irish high crosses, they are generally absent in Pictish sculpture. A possible exception is the two-wheeled vehicle with spoked wheels and railed sides which appeared on a lost stone from Meigle, Perthshire. This was

Figure 41 Sueno's stone in Moray is an outstandingly tall slab (6.5 m), probably dating from the tenth century and commemorating a battle. In the centre are executed prisoners and what may be a broch. Foot soldiers and cavalry are also shown. Traditionally believed to depict a victory over the Vikings, the stone may represent the defeat of the Scottish king Dubh in 966. (Photo: David Longley)

Figure 42 Wheeled vehicle with an awning, which appeared on a stone (now lost) from Meigle, Perthshire (known as Meigle No. 10). It is unlike any other vehicle known in the Celtic world and may be derived from a Roman processional wagon known as a *carpentum*. (Drawing: David Longley, after Anderson, 1881)

drawn by two horses with braided tails and there were two figures as well as the driver. What appears to be an awning was stretched over the vehicle, suggesting that it was not a chariot as such but something more closely related to a 'carpentum', a Roman processional cart.

It is fairly clear that much of the Pictish strength lay in their naval power. No Pictish boat has as yet come to light (though it has been postulated that some of the timbers in the rampart at Portknockie, Banff, could have been re-used from a boat). A Pictish cross slab from Cossans, Angus (known as St Orland's stone), shows what appears to be a plank-built vessel with high prow and stern. A rudder is shown and there are traces on the weathered stone of what appear to be oars. Five figures sit in the boat and are apparently transporting a cross-slab with pointed top, not unlike the Nigg and Aberlemno stones. The slab probably dates from the later eighth century. It stands on a knoll over-looking what was then marsh or water. The might of the Pictish fleet is alluded to in the Annals of Tigernach, and it is not unreasonable to associate some of the coastal promontory forts, such as Portknockie, with its operation.

The fleet of Dalriada is better understood through the muster that survives in the Senchus fer nAlban. The picture that emerges from this is of a warship with seven benches, and seven oars on each side. This was a comparatively small vessel, though some seem to have been bigger. It appears to have been of curragh type – a wooden framework covered with hides. A reference in Adomnan's Life of Columba mentions a leather covering on a boat with oars and a sail, probably raised on a mast stepped amidships. Adomnan also mentions rigging and sail yards, and a reference to Columba and his sailors emptying a bailing well. Another text of the period mentions a certain Conaig being drowned in a wicker boat in AD 622. Gildas, writing about the arrival of the Anglo-Saxons, told how they arrived in curragh-type vessels and described them as 'black', perhaps a reference to the pitch used to make

Figure 43 St Orland's stone, which stands on high ground that once overlooked marsh or water at Cossans, Angus. This carries the only representation of a boat in Pictish art but, unfortunately, is very worn. The boat appears to be a skin-covered vessel with oars and rudder. The shape on the right may be a stone, but is more probably a figure. Height of whole stone: 3 m. (Photo: Tom Gray)

them watertight rather than a moral judgement as once assumed. In the Iona Chronicle, an entry for AD 737 refers to a crew of twenty-two professional sailors. The Senchus relates that each one of twenty houses in Dalriada had to provide twenty-eight oarsmen, that is, the crew for two seven-bench ships.

Adomnan refers to a substantial fifty-five voyages, including several from Scotland to Ireland and one each to Orkney and Pictland.

Traders

Professor Leslie Alcock has recently pointed out that major forts in Dark Age Britain are located close to the sea, in contrast to the pattern of fort-building in the pre-Roman Iron Age when inland locations were more often chosen. These Dark Age forts were probably the centres for the redistribution of merchandise, some of which came directly from the Mediterranean in ships that acquired some of their cargo in the west Mediterranean before sailing on to Britain. This Mediterranean trade brought imported pottery – red slipped dishes of various types known in Britain simply as 'A Ware'. This emanated from a variety of centres but particularly from Tunisia. Large storage 'amphorae' from the east Mediterranean are known as 'B Ware'. 'Mortaria' (grinding bowls) for food from the Bordeaux region are known as 'D Ware'. Bordeaux may have sent wine, perhaps in wooden casks. Trade with the Mediterranean seems to have been ultimately from Byzantium by way of the Atlantic seaboard and thence through the Irish Sea. It began in the later fifth century and continued during the sixth. Mediterranean pottery travelled as far north as Dalriada, but does not seem to have penetrated Pictland.

A second boom in overseas trade brought other merchandise to northern Scotland from the late sixth century onwards. A variety of forms of pottery in a gritty fabric, E ware, was traded from somewhere between the Loire and the Seine. It continued to be imported during the seventh and into much of the eighth century. In the sixth to seventh centuries the trade in pottery was supplemented by glass vessels from Gaul. Glass and E Ware tend to occur on the same sites. Glassware came in as complete vessels but later, reduced to cullet, may have been used for making beads or enamel. The trade in glass vessels seems to have been concentrated in the west, reaching Dalriada but apparently not Pictland. The vessel glass from Dundurn along with its E Ware is regarded as being the result of redistribution from Dalriada. Which commodities were traded in return for the pottery and glass is not known. As Alcock has pointed out, they are likely to have been items regarded as luxuries. He has suggested sable, ermine and other white furs, freshwater pearls and eider-down. He proposed that forts such as Dundurn and Dunadd, with their industrial functions (see later, p. 87), should be seen as the equivalent of the North Sea, Baltic and Channel trading bases, similar in function to places such as Hamwih (Southampton) in Anglo-Saxon England.

Not all trade was far-flung; finds from Dunadd point to trade with Northumbria. The range of materials represented in the finds from excavated sites suggests a local trade network. A few Irish objects from Dunadd might indicate trade with Ireland, and among the finds from Jorvik (Viking York) was part of a Pictish penannular brooch of the eighth century.

Figure 44 Some typical reconstructed vessels in E Ware. This is a type of gritty, coarse pottery, usually in oatmeal colours, which was imported to Scotland and Ireland from the end of the sixth century until the eighth. It may have originated in the Bordeaux region of France and is well represented at Dunadd. (Drawing: L. Laing)

Economy

Both the Picts and the Scots were essentially farmers. The evidence from Dundurn showed that sixty-one per cent of the bones found were from cattle, thirty-one per cent from pig and only eight per cent from sheep or goat. The cattle were small, and most seem to have lived for more than two-and-a-half years, suggesting that autumn slaughter of much of the stock was not practised. Virtually all the bones from Dundurn were of domesticated animals, the only exceptions being those from two deer and a heron. From Dunollie in Dalriada the bone assemblage again contained the greatest proportion from cattle (sixty-four per cent), then pig (nineteen per cent), then sheep/goat (seventeen per cent). At Dunollie the sheep seem to have been slaughtered under the age of eighteen months, suggesting they were kept for meat rather than wool. Wild animals were again poorly represented: from red deer only antlers were found and from fish only three bones. Horses, which figure prominently on Pictish sculptures, were represented by only two bones.

Buckquoy in Orkney produced abundant bone material from its Pictish phase, as well as from the Norse. About seven thousand bones were recovered. These comprised those from cattle (fifty per cent), sheep (thirty per cent) and pig (twenty per cent). One third of these animals died in their first year of life, thus meat was clearly of greater importance than wool. A certain amount of line-fishing was practised in Pictish times, but fishing was more important for the Norse.

Dunollie produced no evidence for cereal production, apart from a quern for grinding grain. Grains of oats and barley were present at Dundurn and Birsay, and these crops are also attested at Dunadd. At Dundurn, cultivation seems to have been carried out on terraces below the fort. The introduction of terrace farming has been attributed to Northumbrian influence. Also at Dundurn, wild cherries, raspberries and hazelnuts were gathered for food. Bracken was collected for bedding and litter, and mosses as an equivalent of lavatory paper.

In general terms, cattle were clearly the most important element in the economy of the Picts and Scots, as they were in contemporary Ireland. Slaughter seems to have been carried out near to where the meat was going to be eaten, and grain was ground with rotary querns, though the older type of saddle quern is known from Dunadd.

Costume

Clothes, with the exception of a certain amount of leatherwork, have not survived, but a reasonable impression of Pictish costume can be derived from representations on sculptures.

Women do not figure prominently on sculpture, but a female is shown on a stone from Monifeith, Angus. Here she appears to be wearing a long skirt and some kind of cloak, with a single penannular brooch with the terminals facing downwards (the opposite of a representation of the wearing of a penannular brooch on an Irish high cross). Her hair is short, but bunched at the side of her head. Another woman is riding side-saddle on the Hilton of Cadboll stone. She too has a similarly positioned penannular brooch on her breast and a long skirt with some kind of cloak or over-mantle. Her hair is worn shoulder-length.

Of the male representations, many seem to wear hooded cloaks, reminiscent of the *byrrus britannicus* for which Roman Britain was famous, and which can be seen on some Romano-British sculptures. The figure on the Golspie stone wears a short tunic, as does that on the Rhynie stone and others on a diversity of other sculptures of various dates. Clearly the tunic was fairly universally worn. It was frequently covered by a cloak and, in the case of a figure on horseback on a stone from Kirriemuir, some kind of pectoral or shoulder cape. The long toga-like garment worn by David on the St Andrews shrine is probably inspired by a Classical manuscript model and thus would not be typical of Pictland. Pictish men seem to have grown beards and moustaches, and their hair is worn long, often reaching well down their backs. Shorter hair is also found. A cleric depicted on a stone at Invergowrie wears a long vestment and has a short tonsure. The long robe of Daniel on Meigle No. 2 is probably inspired by a Mediterranean model. The three warriors on the stone from Birsay, Orkney, however, wear ankle-length robes that do not appear to be derived from an exotic model, and two of these figures seem to have their hair tied back with headbands. The variations in costume and hairstyle on Pictish stones may reflect rank.

Apart from penannular brooches, there are stick pins from Pictland which were probably used either as hair-pins or as clothes fasteners. One of the finest is a silver example from Golspie, Sutherland, with the head taking the form of that of a worried Pict.

Figure 45 Silver pin, found in a private garden at Golspie, Sutherland, probably eighth century. Such dress-pins were used for fastening clothing. Human heads are rare (though they occur on a few Irish pins), and the furrowed brow of this Pict is similar to that on the heads on the Portsoy (Banff) whetstone (see Figure 92). Length: 6 cm. (Photo: Royal Museums of Scotland)

Craftspeople and Industrial Workers

A wide range of crafts and minor industrial activities are attested from the major excavated forts, though of course it is not certain to what extent the forts were the foci for such activities. Most sites, however, produce evidence for some crafts, and it would seem that some skills at least were widely distributed in the population.

Large numbers of objects must have been made of organic materials which have therefore not survived. Sculptures show a variety of everyday articles, including a two-seater bench with carved terminals and a high back on the reverse of a stone from Aldbar, and chairs with animal terminals and stretchers on the Dunfallandy stone. A cauldron with two ring handles is shown suspended from a metal tripod or other frame on the Glamis Manse stone. Tools, including tongs, anvils, hammers and various types of axe, appear on various stones.

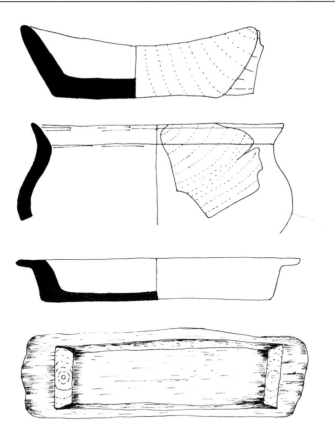

Figure 46 The crannog at Loch Glashan, Argyll, produced a variety of finds, including leatherwork and woodwork. The wooden vessels are a useful reminder of how much was made in this material but is now lost. Typical of the finds are this dish and lathe-turned bowl. Dish length: 70 cm; bowl diameter: 15.3 cm. (Drawing: Amanda Straw, after Earwood)

Weaving is not well represented in the lands of the Picts and Scots. Spindle whorls (for weighting the spindle) are not very abundant finds, and pin-beaters (for packing down threads on a loom) and weaving combs are absent after AD 200, though a bone pin from Dundurn might be a pin-beater.

Woodworking is attested in the sixth to eighth centuries from the crannog at Loch Glashan, Argyll, where waterlogging preserved a variety of items. Perhaps the most interesting were wooden containers,

Figure 47 Wooden box, found near Birsay, Orkney, filled with tools. The tools were more appropriate to leatherworking than woodworking, and it is thought that the carving was done by someone who was not in the habit of working with wood. The box shows how Celtic designs must have been used to decorate all kinds of materials in the eighth century. Length: 30 cm. (Photo: Royal Museums of Scotland)

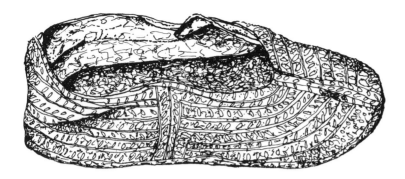

Figure 48 Decorated leather shoe, probably seventh or early eighth century. This was just one of the variety of finds resulting from the excavations at Dundurn, Perthshire. Length: 23 cm. (Drawing: Amanda Straw, after L. Alcock)

carved out of blocks of wood. The largest measured 9.55 cm long and was rectangular with carrying handles at each end. There were smaller troughs, also with lugs in one case, and a turned wooden bowl which showed that the lathe was in use, in this case to make a vessel not unlike an E Ware bowl. Spatulas, pegs, pins, handles, wedges, a spindle, a spindle whorl and a paddle (the latter possibly used in beating textile fibres) were recovered. Dundurn also produced a badly made handled bowl or ladle, and remains of wattle flooring. A box, richly carved with curvilinear Celtic patterns and containing tools, was found at Birsay, Orkney. The carving of the box and the nature of the tools suggest that it belonged to a leatherworker rather than a carpenter.

Little leatherwork has survived, with the exception of a shoe from Dundurn. This is of one-piece construction with an all-over stamped design. It was of very high quality and without exact parallel, though leather shoes of the period are known from Ireland. The leatherwork from Loch Glashan included part of a tunic or jerkin, shoes and knife-sheaths. Shoes are also represented in sculptures.

Figure 49 Bone comb, found in the dun at Dun Cuier, Barra, seventh or eighth century. Combs used by the early Christian Celts included composite double-sided varieties, and single-sided examples, sometimes with ornate backs. Such combs appear in stylized form as Pictish symbols. This example may owe something to the Frisian combs of the fifth century. Length: 7.1 cm. (Photo: Royal Museums of Scotland)

Bonework is fairly well represented, mostly in the form of dress-pins, needles and awls or points. A bone spoon and a knife-handle were among the finds from Buckquoy. The most common artefacts made from bone, apart from pins, were combs, of which there are two main varieties. One has a single line of teeth, the other is double-sided. These are often composite, with strengthening plates fastened on with bronze rivets. Sometimes the combs are decorated, usually with simple ring-and-dot ornament. Some, such as one from Buckquoy, may have been suspended from a belt.

Stone was used for whetstones, ingot moulds, pot lids and querns.

The Celts do not seem to have produced glass, but imported glass was melted down to make a variety of beads and bracelets. Many of the beads are very attractive, with different coloured glass in strands – one from Dunadd contrasts yellow, black and white. The finest piece of glasswork, however, is a stud (or boss) from Dundurn, with swirls of white and dark brown glass, inlaid with five discs of glass, and surmounted by five smaller bosses with white and blue spirals. Such ornament is found on some Irish beads, and the boss from Dundurn could have come from Dalriada. It might have been from a reliquary, but was more probably simply a playing piece.

The main crafts were those of the smiths. Iron was worked in bowl furnaces. A blacksmith's tongs, hammer and anvil appear as Pictish symbols. Ironworking is not represented in the small area excavated at Dundurn, but is at Dunadd. Iron was fashioned into a wide variety of objects. Among the most interesting are barrel padlocks from Dundurn, and arrowheads, arrowtips, woodman's axes, chisels, awls, hammerheads, knives, nails, loops, strips, handles and rods from Dunollie. A similar range of finds have been made at Dunadd, with the addition of a few pieces of Irish type, including a slotted-topped object, a socketed object with three prongs, and a saw. Iron was absent from Buckquoy.

Figure 50 Multi-coloured stud from Dundurn, Perthshire. This may have been used to decorate metalwork or could have been a playing piece for a game. Although the Dark Age Celts did not make glass, they worked imported glass into beads, bracelets and studs. Width: 1.5 cm. (Drawing: Amanda Straw, after L. Alcock)

Figure 51 Iron objects from Dunadd, Argyll. These comprise a spearhead, a knife with bone handle and two saws. Heights: 17.2 cm, 7.8 cm, 15.5 cm, 5.4 cm. (Drawing: Amanda Straw)

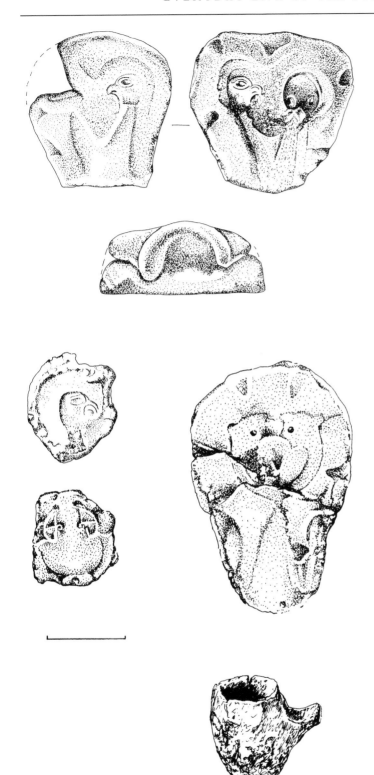

Figure 52 Moulds from Birsay, Orkney. Ornamental bronzework was cast in two-piece moulds which were only used once. Complex objects were sometimes made in sections. The pair of moulds (top) came from a Pictish workshop which seems to have specialized in producing fine penannular brooches. The two sections are keyed to facilitate fitting. Actual size. Also shown (bottom) is a typical small triangular crucible with a lug for the tongs to grasp in pouring. This came from the same site. Width: 4.9 cm. (Drawings: Gwen Seller and Amanda Straw)

Ornamental bronzework is extremely well attested by clay moulds, crucibles and metalwork debris. Most crucibles seem to have been small and triangular, but deeper cylindrical types are also represented, as well as some with knobs to facilitate lifting. Clay moulds for bronze-casting have been found at Dundurn, Dunollie, Dunadd, Clatchard Craig, Craig Phadrig and Birsay (see later, p. 85ff). Clearly, ornamental metalwork was produced at all the high-status sites. Whether this was done by resident craftsmen or itinerants (the latter is less likely) is not known. The moulds were made in two pieces, keyed with a knife- point or with some other projection and indentation to enable them to be correctly positioned. The metal was poured in through a funnel-shaped ingate, produced in the mould with a wood or bone 'former'. The moulds appear to have been used only once. In the case of simple objects such as pins, an actual bone pin might be used as a model to form the mould. In the case of more complex objects a model may also have been used, with details added by engraving or stamping with a die on to the soft clay. The moulds were probably set on edge in sand while the metal was poured in, and the finished castings trimmed and in some cases further decorated with engraving. Complex objects were made in sections and then put together. For example, three-dimensional bird heads were cast at Birsay, probably for attachment to penannular brooches. Plain studs, buckles, pins, finger rings and penannular brooches are the objects most commonly represented among the moulds. The most ornate are the series from Birsay, for casting penannular brooches with bird-head terminals and interlace decoration. Interlaced penannulars were also produced at Clatchard Craig and Dunadd. The smelting was done in bowl furnaces, and the bellows nozzle, which would have been of wood, was protected by a clay sleeve (tuyère), fragments of which have been found.

Lead also was worked, and there are traces of gold on crucibles from Dunadd, as well as pieces of goldwork from Dunadd and Dunollie. A lead disc from Birsay with a complex triskele decoration could either have been a motif-piece to try out the design, or used as a die for stamped silver or in lost-wax casting. Examples of motif pieces have come from Dunadd (where the designs include one for a penannular brooch) and Birsay (where a bone had a complex design for a chip-carved ornament). A mould from Dundurn also seems to have been experimental.

Figure 53 Lead 'trial-piece' from Birsay, Orkney. This item bears the negative for a design known as the Durrow spiral and may have been used in making moulds. Diameter: 5 cm. The design is most frequently found on the mounts for hanging bowls that have been discovered in Anglo-Saxon graves of the sixth and early seventh centuries. (Drawing: Gwen Seller)

Pastimes

Riders are common on sculptures, and from the depictions it is possible to establish that horses were ridden both bareback and with saddles, sometimes with elaborate long saddle-cloths, for example on Meigle No. 4. Harness is shown, as are bits with side rings, but there is no sign that stirrups were used.

There is evidence of board games. Bone knobs with metal shanks, often identified as pins, may instead have been pieces to move around a board with peg holes. These are attested at Clatchard Craig.

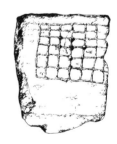

Figrue 54 Board game from Dun Chonallaich, Argyll. A variety of board games was probably played by the Picts and Scots. This one, which has counterparts from Buckquoy, Orkney, was probably for an Irish combat game called branduth. (Drawing: Amanda Straw)

Figure 55 Musical instruments on Pictish and Scottish sculptures from Dunkeld, Barochan, Monifeith and Dupplin. (Drawing: David Longley)

Music is represented by depictions of instruments on Pictish and Scottish sculptures. Harps are of two types: large instruments which stand on the ground, similar to those in use today, and smaller instruments. Large harps are depicted on the Dupplin cross, Nigg, Monifieth (Pictish) and Ardchattan (Scottic). These are the earliest examples of true harps known in Europe. Blast horns appear on occasion, for example at Barochan. A triple pipe, probably a terminal horn, appears on the Ardchattan stone and on a stone from Lethandy, Perthshire. The latter also shows what may be a barrel drum. On the Nigg slab, a figure appears to have cymbals, though this instrument may be borrowed from a manuscript model.

Drinking was clearly a favoured pursuit. The Picts are attributed in legend with the discovery of heather ale, and a Pict drinks from a drinking horn with bird-head terminal on a stone from Bullion, Invergowrie.

The Settlements of the Iron Age in northern Scotland

Both the Picts and the Scots followed traditional farming and building methods that had been favoured for many centuries. It cannot be stressed too strongly that there was no major cultural break in Scotland

Figure 56 A drinking Pict in shallow relief adorns a slab from Bullion, Invergowrie, Angus. Typically Pictish is the small round shield worn from a strap around the neck. The drinking horn has a bird-head terminal, an example of which is known from Ireland, but the head has been angled so that it regards the drinker, perhaps as a joke. (Photo: Royal Museums of Scotland)

from the end of the Bronze Age through to the Middle Ages. Throughout this long period of time (nearly two millennia) there was, however, some minor regional variation, as types of monument evolved or fell from favour. There is a marked regionalism, with some measure of unity being observable in the Atlantic province of the northern and western isles and north Scottish mainland, with a further coherence in the second main cultural province, that of the north-east.

Ideally, historically identifiable peoples should leave easily recognizable material remains for study. These, typically, should be found in the areas where the people lived with occasional outliers or exports, and within contexts clearly datable to the periods in which they flourished. The Picts rarely conform to this model. There are no typically or indisputably Pictish artefacts or settlement types (unless the figure-of-eight houses of Orkney and the Hebrides are accepted as Pictish), and the most definitive features of 'Pictishness' are to be found only in their art (see Chapter 4). This underlines a feature of modern and past life that we have frequently commented upon – that 'political' changes or 'national' groupings can exist perfectly well without dramatic modifications to lifestyle.

Thus, while ideas and attitudes can bind a population together and be witnessed through language and art, there may be nothing to distinguish the people from those with quite different attitudes and ideas. Since small subsistence-level economies without strong import/export links or central governments are being dealt with here primarily, there will be very little evidence to consider.

The landscape of northern Scotland changed remarkably little during the period of the Picts and their prehistoric forebears. Similarly, economy and population were basically static, though increasingly from the second century AD it is possible to chart the growth of population and the rise of new centres of power.

Between c. BC 900 and 500 there had been some changes in prehistoric Scotland. Contacts were established between north-east Scotland and the north European mainland, and there were changes in settlement types. Among the innovations were hillforts – hilltop settlements defended by one or more ramparts. The earliest were timber-laced and made their appearance in the seventh century BC at a time when the bronze industry in northern Scotland was particularly flourishing. Such timber-laced forts are fairly widespread, but the greatest concentration is in the heart of what became Pictland, in central and eastern Scotland and the Moray Firth. Here their recognition has probably been helped by the fact that in cases where the timbers in the ramparts were fired, the nature of the stone was such that it had a comparatively low melting point and in some cases has fused into a slaggy mass. The burning horizontal timbers caused draught channels which acted as bellows and heated the core of the rampart to a high degree. These vitrified forts were once seen as the product of deliberate firing to strengthen the wall core, but they are now more widely regarded as the accidental

products of conflagrations. The timber-laced forts probably had a relatively short life since repairs to the timbers were almost impossible, but
finds from excavated examples suggest that they were being constructed
until the fourth century BC, if not later.

Apart from these forts there were other, probably mostly later types
of simpler farmsteads within enclosures. Generally they comprised a
low rampart and ditch. These were intended not so much for defence
as to keep animals and children from straying out, or marauding animals from straying in.

Souterrains

Common on open settlements are souterrains. These are underground
passages usually lined with stone and connected with above-ground
huts. The earliest known souterrain was excavated at Douglasmuir,
Angus, where it was found to be no more than an under-floor passageway, datable to before BC 500. From such beginnings, souterrains
proper evolved. Although they fell out of use in the second century
AD, before the Picts are named in historical records, the souterrains are
distributed in what became historical Pictland and are found on settlements which had a long life from the pre-Roman Iron Age through to
the sixth century AD, or even later.

Perhaps the best evidence for the nature of souterrains and their
associated settlements comes from Newmill, Perthshire. Here the main
occupation of the settlement and use of the souterrain started around
the first century BC and continued until the second century AD, with
occupation of the site continuing until the eighth. The souterrain was
stone-walled and floored, but probably had a wooden pitched roof
which projected, along with part of the wall, above ground level. The
excavators suggested that it was entered from the adjacent hut by
means of a ramp which led down to a subterranean door. A side opening enabled exit or entrance from outside the house. The souterrain
was curved, ranging between 2.5 and 4 m wide, and the passage was 20 m
long. The settlement produced evidence of grain-grinding and ironworking, and a scatter of animal bones, but no artefacts of note. The
excavators considered that the souterrain was used either for religious
activities, or, much more probably, as a store. It was estimated that it
could store more food than a family would need for a year. The house
to which it was attached was bigger than the others without souterrains
on the settlement, measuring 17.6 m in diameter. It was suggested that
its souterrain could have served as the store for all the houses in the
community. It may or may not be fanciful to suggest that here is the
evidence for the 'holes in the ground' in which the Picts traditionally
had their siesta. Recent work suggests that, after the souterrains fell out
of use in the second century, houses on the same sites sometimes had
sunken floors, perhaps further lending support to the legend.

Souterrains are widespread in Pictland, though outliers occur in southern Scotland where it has been claimed they were built by refugees from further north. In all about two hundred are known, with concentrations in Fife and Angus, Perthshire, Aberdeenshire, Sutherland, Ross and Cromarty, Skye and the Outer Hebrides, and in the northern isles. Some were more sophisticated than the Newmill example. In Orkney the Rennibister souterrain had a corbelled roof to its main chamber, while the Grain earth-house was roofed with stone slabs.

Atlantic Scotland

A separate cultural tradition is observable in the Atlantic province of Iron Age Scotland, that is the northern and western isles, and Scottish mainland north and west of the Caledonian Canal. This is the province of the brochs, popularly known in Scotland as 'Picts' houses'.

More debate has surrounded the study of brochs in Scotland than almost any other aspect of Scottish archaeology. These are certainly a major feature of the northern landscape. Enough survive sufficiently well to show they were drystone towers with a single entrance, usually flanked by guard-chambers in the thickness of the wall, with hollow walling, internal staircases and internal timber ranges. In contrast to the rest of Iron Age Scotland, the Atlantic region has produced a comparative abundance of artefacts which has enabled archaeologists to build up a fuller picture of the life of the broch builders and users.

There are about five hundred brochs in Scotland. Many were probably quite low towers, but some more elaborate examples have

Figure 57 The Broch of Mousa, Shetland. This is the best-preserved of all the Iron Age broch towers of Atlantic Scotland. Still standing 13.1 m high, it was built around the first century AD and was later used as a refuge by an eloping Viking couple. (Photo: Scottish Development Department)

survived. The Broch of Mousa, for instance, which is the best preserved, stands 13 m today, and originally must have been at least 15 m high. Its diameter is 15.2 m, of which a surprising amount is taken up by the width of the wall. Other well-preserved tall examples include Dun Telve and Dun Troddan in Inverness-shire, and Dun Carloway on Lewis.

Of the many different theories that have been advanced about broch origins, the one currently favoured is that they evolved out of round, stone-built houses current in Orkney from around BC 700. Brochs

Figure 58 Broch of Gurness, Aikerness, Orkney. Excavated before the Second World War, this broch, flanked by a kennel for a guard-dog, and further defended by a ditch, rises out of the midst of a village of stone-built subrectangular huts. The site was later occupied by the Vikings. (Photo: L. Laing)

Figure 59 A view of the broch village at Aikerness, Orkney. (Photo: L. Laing)

were the result of trying to make these undefended, round, isolated houses more monumental. The first stage in the development of brochs involved the building of more complex round houses, which happened between BC 400 and 200. These had some features of broch architecture. From BC 200 onwards, true brochs evolved. They became the centres of 'villages' which clustered round them, perhaps numbering thirty to forty families, well exemplified by Gurness, Aikerness, on the Orkney Mainland, where approach to the broch was by way of a long path through the buildings it dwarfed. From Orkney the brochs spread to other parts of the Atlantic province and, although the brochs themselves fell out of use in the early centuries AD, the sites continued to be occupied until the arrival of the Vikings, that is, throughout the Pictish period.

Life of the Broch Builders

It is probably fairly reasonable to infer a role not unlike that of medieval clan chiefs for the broch builders, occupying their castle-like brochs in splendour while their followers looked up at the 'big hoose'. A hint that times were turbulent is perhaps provided by two hands, severed at the wrist, still wearing spiral finger rings. These were found in a midden at the Broch of Gurness, though the accoutrements of war are generally absent from broch sites. Some painted pebbles may have been slingshot, the painted designs perhaps being tribal or designed to ensure they reached their mark. Socketted bone points are also found. These may have served as spears and been attached to wooden hafts with flammable material to make fire spears. Instead of weapons, broch sites produced a diversity of subsistence equipment suited to the needs of a farming community with, in particular, an array of bone artefacts and stone rubbers. These serve as a reminder that Atlantic Scotland lay just outside the very conservative 'Circumpolar Zone' in which bone and stone artefact types and even pottery underwent only modest changes over long periods of time. Ironworking seems to have been carried out on some broch sites in the surrounding settlement, for example at Midhowe on the Orcadian island of Rousay. Bronzework is attested by triangular crucibles and moulds for making such simple objects as stick-pins. Much of the bonework was specialist equipment for the weaving and sewing of textiles – pin beaters and weaving combs, spindle whorls, bobbins and slotted bones. The dark interiors of the brochs were lit by stone lamps, and the long winter evenings were whiled away playing games with long dice. In the absence of wood, stone furniture was fashioned, built-in cupboards being among the features of the broch huts. Roman artefacts – pottery, beads, glass and the occasional coin – indicate the high status of the broch owners.

Forts and Farms of the Picts

It is significant that around the second century AD there were substantial changes in the territories that later became Pictland that do not seem to represent any major change in the population, but which more probably reflect political upheavals. For example, in north-east Scotland there are signs of an emerging wealthy patronage which was able to afford sumptuous metalwork. Starting perhaps in the last years of the first century AD, and continuing certainly through the second and probably later still, there flourished, in the area centred on Aberdeenshire, a tradition of ornamental metalwork. This has been termed 'Caledonian' and shows affinities with the 'Brigantian' tradition. The latter flourished in Yorkshire in the later first century as a last fling of Brigantian tribal independence before the Roman conquest. The Caledonian smiths were skilled in producing massive bronze armlets with high relief modelling involving slender, confronted trumpet patterns. Some of the finest of these also carry enamelwork in their terminals. They were clearly high-status objects, as were the snake-headed heavy bracelets of the type found at Culbin Sands, Moray, and the mouthpiece of the 'carnyx' (boar's head trumpet) found at Deskford in Banff. Such instruments appear on Iron Age Celtic coins and seem to have been brandished as rallying standards in battle.

In the same period the use of souterrains appears to have come to an end. Most of the excavated souterrains were deliberately dismantled and filled in, though the sites on which they are found continued in occupation. It has been suggested that this was due to the rise of new centres of power with greater wealth than previously: the souterrains had become too small for the quantities of produce stored in them. That cannot, of course, be proved, but there are other clues to growing centres of power and wealth in Pictland.

One of these indicators is Roman merchandize. It has been noticed that on the Continent, beyond the Roman frontiers, Roman goods penetrated far. At first, as one might imagine, the distribution became more thinly scattered as artefacts travelled from the frontier. In due course, however, the merchandize was collected in centres, where it had a status value for the chiefs based there. This has been viewed as part of a wider political scenario and the emergence of new chiefdoms among the early Germans.

In Scotland the Roman merchandize reaching native sites did not comprise mundane, everyday items but high-status commodities: gold or high-quality silver coins, top-quality Roman Samian pottery and Roman glass. The presence of Roman material of this kind on souterrain sites suggests that the sites were of high status. A few burials of the second century with Roman material have been found: one from Tarland, Aberdeenshire, had Roman playing pieces; at Airlie and Kingoldrum in Angus there were glass vessels; at Westray in Orkney there was a glass cup; and from a burial (or possibly a ritual deposit) at

Cairnhill, Monquhitter, Aberdeenshire, there was a Roman gemstone. Roman artefacts occur on broch sites, as has already been noted, and it is likely that the large hoard of Roman denarii found at Falkirk constituted a buy-off payment to one of the tribes to the north of the Antonine Wall in the period 160–230. In short, chiefs in Caledonia were becoming rich and powerful through Roman pay-offs. It is plain from historical sources that such pay-offs occurred in the fourth century; it is little wonder, therefore, that the Romans did not take kindly to the Picts.

However, despite these indications of a rise in Pictish fortunes, settlement types that reflect population distribution and make-up changed remarkably little during this period. Some types, notably the forts with timber-laced ramparts which began in the middle of the first millennium BC, continued, albeit with a break in occupation in most cases, into the time of the Dark Age Picts, and overlapped with open farmsteads. It is clear that, despite new political groupings or affiliations, the basic population remained constant.

The pattern of settlement observable in northern Scotland in the Iron Age remained as diverse in the time of the Picts. It has already been noted (see p. 21) that place-names suggest much of Pictland remained densely wooded, and, as the mountain regions were not much suited to farming, settlement seems to have been concentrated in Fife, Angus and the lowland coastal strip around the east coast into Aberdeenshire and Moray. The distribution of Pictish carved stones (see Chapter 4) and Pit- names probably gives a fairly accurate indication of the main areas of settlement. Within this general area, a detailed study of southern Pictland (mainly Fife and Angus) has suggested that the distribution of Class I Pictish symbol stones relates more closely to the distribution of hillforts in the region than to good arable land. From this it has been deduced that in the period in which the Class I stones were being erected (i.e. probably mainly before AD 700), the centres of power were focused on hillforts. In contrast, in the period when Class II stones were being erected (in the main in the eighth and ninth centuries), there was a move away from the hillforts and towards new foci. There are also signs of a shift in importance northwards from the south, and to settlement on good arable land.

This would seem to fit in with what can be inferred from other sources about the changing political structure within Pictland. From the late second century onwards, souterrains, which it was suggested had grown too small for the produce now stored in them, were abandoned. This points to larger political groupings, and almost coincidentally with this it is possible to observe the re-occupation of some Iron Age fort sites and the building of some forts *ab initio*. In the North the brochs seem to have declined in importance. However, just as the lowland settlements which had previously had souterrains continued in use, probably into the Viking Age, so did the broch sites in Atlantic Scotland, implying an underlying continuity of population and settlement.

Figure 60 Dun, Strathtay.
Typical of southern Pictland are
the stone-walled forts or duns, of
which a concentration can be
found in Strathtay, Perthshire.
They are probably mostly of the
Iron Age, but some may have
been occupied in the time of
the Picts. (Photo: L. Laing)

The fort-occupying phase of Pictish history extends from perhaps the third century, or certainly the fourth, through to the eighth. This roughly corresponds with the period of re-use of forts in other parts of Britain, notably in south Wales and south-west England. The question that has to be asked is whether the hillfort-building phase of Pictish history was simply part of a widespread trend, perhaps prompted by wider economic and political factors in western Europe, or whether it was a direct response to trends within Pictland itself. The answer is probably both. The immediate causes of the larger political groupings within Pictland were probably growing unification against the Roman threat to the south, and increased prosperity due to improved climate and farming methods. Outside Pictland in other parts of the 'Celtic' world, similar benefits were being felt from improved farm production and climate, and new political configurations were an indirect response to Rome as much as to the increased prosperity.

A major obstacle to studying the settlement archaeology of Pictland is the dearth of adequately excavated sites. It is very easy to read too much into the few sites that have been scientifically examined in recent times, and thereby to obtain a distorted picture. One of the largest forts in north-east Scotland, Tap o' Noth, has never been excavated. The summit is encircled by a massive vitrified wall, presumably belonging to

PLATE 1 The Antonine Wall, begun by Antoninus Pius in AD142 to defend Britannia from the northern tribes, was built of turf on a stone foundation, with a deep, wide ditch in front, still visible here, near Falkirk, Stirlingshire. (Photo: David Paterson)

PLATE 2 The Celtic hermitage at Sgor Nam Ban-Naoimha ('The Crag of the Holy Women') on the Hebridean island of Canna. (Photo: Eric Talbot)

PLATE 4 The Hunterston brooch, an outstanding example of seventh-century ornamental metalwork from Dalriada. (© The Trustees of the National Museums of Scotland 1993)

PLATE 3 The *Christi autem* page (Matthew 1.18) from the Book of Kells, one of the finest Insular gospel books, probably produced on Iona in the late eighth century. (Trinity College Library, Dublin, MS 58, f. 34r)

PLATE 5 The monastic site at Iona. (Photo: David Paterson)

PLATE 6 Loch Shira, Argyll. (Photo: David Paterson)

PLATE 7 A pre-second-century house and souterrain at Ardestie, Angus, typical of many found in southern Pictland. (Photo: David Longley)

PLATE 8 A 'carpet page' from the seventh-century Book of Durrow, displaying motifs also found on contemporary metalwork. (Trinity College Library, Dublin, MS 57, f. 192v)

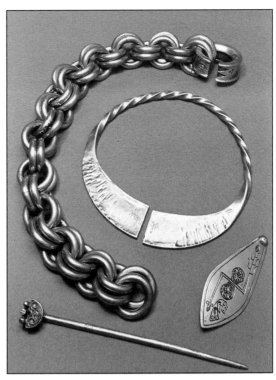

PLATE 9 Examples of Pictish silverwork of the fifth to seventh century. The chain, from Newmachar, Aberdeenshire, was probably the chain of office of a Pictish king. The brooch and the plaque decorated with Pictish symbols are from the hoard found at Norrie's Law, Fife. The ornate hand-pin is from Gaulcross, Banff. (© The Trustees of the National Museums of Scotland 1993)

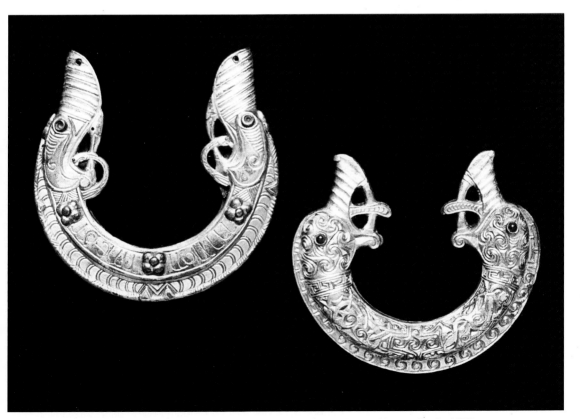

PLATE 10 Eighth-century silver sword chapes from St Ninian's Isle, Shetland. (© The Trustees of the National Museums of Scotland 1993)

PLATE 11 This reliquary from Monymusk, the only complete example found in Britain, held a relic of St Columba; it was carried into battle at Bannockburn in 1314 (© The Trustees of the National Museums of Scotland 1993)

PLATE 12 Looking east across Aberdeenshire towards the sea from the fortifications at Bennachie. (Photo: Jim Henderson)

PLATE 13 The Pictish cross-slab from Hilton of Cadboll, Ross, dating from around 800, displays a Pictish hunting scene bordered by an inhabited vine scroll with Anglo-Saxon affinities (© The Trustees of the National Museums of Scotland 1993)

PLATE 14 Rising behind this Pictish symbol stone at Rhynie can be seen Tap o' Noth, one of the largest Iron Age hillforts in north-east Scotland. (Photo: Jim Henderson)

Figure 61 A classic example of a vitrified fort, Tap o' Noth, Aberdeenshire. Here timber-laced ramparts have been fired, resulting in the core fusing to a slaggy mass. Although such forts were a feature of the earlier Iron Age (seventh to fifth centuries BC), some at least were re-occupied in Pictish times. (Photo: Jim Henderson)

the period between BC 700 and 400, or thereabouts. However the spill from this seems to overlie a series of hut-circles within a light outer enclosure, which could well belong to the Pictish period. Some of the larger forts appear unfinished, and claims have been made that this is to be accounted for by the Roman advance into north-east Scotland, a suggestion which is unprovable and not very probable. Alongside these large forts is a variety of smaller, but equally undatable forts, often with insubstantial ramparts.

Pictland forts are found at different altitudes and are of different sizes, but one group is characterized by having oblong, timber-laced defences, often, though not always, vitrified. The main fort at Tap o' Noth is of this type, as are those at Finavon and Craig Phadrig. Several of the forts show signs of much larger-scale destruction of their defences than is apparent in other vitrified forts, which might be explained by a deliberate firing of the ramparts. Many, like Tap o' Noth, have outlying enclosures.

An important category of fort in north-east Scotland is found on promontories. These use an earthwork to cut off the promontory and are usually, though not essentially, small. Some of these show signs of first being constructed in the early Iron Age, but having been reoccupied and defended in the Pictish period.

The classic promontory fort is Burghead, Moray, which has not produced any conclusive evidence of use in the pre-Pictish period. At

Figure 62 Burghead, Moray, from the sea. This promontory fort was defended by a rampart with timber-lacing fastened by iron dowels or 'nails'. Probably first built around the fourth century AD, it comprises an upper and a lower fort, extensively built over in the nineteenth century. It was occupied until at least the ninth century. (Photo: David Longley)

Burghead the promontory was defended by a timber-laced rampart, fastened together with iron dowels. Radio-carbon dating suggests that it may have been erected around AD 300. This date might be supported by the discovery on the site of a Roman coin, which probably arrived in the fourth century. Burghead is the largest Pictish fort so far recorded. It was unfortunately built over in the nineteenth century when a series of banks and ditches were destroyed almost completely, but about half of the interior still survives and has been sampled by excavation. The fort has an upper and lower enclosure, defined by ramparts, and the interior extends to nearly three hectares. The timber-laced ramparts of the inner fort had coursed-stone facings, and these seem to have included some of the slabs with bull carvings that are such a feature of Burghead.

Inside the fort is a well of uncertain but probably Pictish date. This is approached by a flight of twenty rock-cut steps, ending in a rock-cut chamber with a central tank bordered by a platform. Various uses have been proposed for the well. It was later associated with the cult of St Ethan, but its Christian use as a baptistry suggests that it had a pagan cult use before the advent of Christianity, rather than merely a practical function of supplying water. An early Christian ecclesiastical site is known nearby. Apparently there were stone foundations of rectangular buildings within the fort, but finds from the nineteenth century investigations are lost, with the exception of a ninth-century Anglo-Saxon mount for a blast horn.

A second promontory fort can be seen at Greencastle, Portknockie. This was first occupied around the ninth century BC. The site was

Figure 63 Rock-cut steps lead down to a well at Burghead, Moray. Possibly originally connected with a water cult, in Christian times the well was dedicated to St Ethan. (Photo: David Longley)

redefended *c.* AD 330 with a timber palisade. This was replaced by a much more substantial timber-framed wall, with squared vertical and horizontal timbers, mostly of oak, set into mortices in the transverse timbers. This framework seems to have been prefabricated, from wood that was in part re-used. This rampart enclosed an area of less than one thousand square metres. The only structure associated with the Pictish fort was a rectilinear building with rounded corners. Such promontory forts may have been connected with the Pictish navy.

Of the other sites in north-east Scotland, mention may be made of Cullykhan, Banff, and Craig Phadrig, Inverness. Cullykhan was an Iron Age vitrified fort, later occupied by Picts. The Pictish evidence comprised a wooden porched structure dated to the early fourth century AD. The date was provided by a wooden object from this structure. Other finds include spindle whorls.

Craig Phadrig near Inverness is a fort believed to be associated with Bridei mac Maelcon. As at Cullykhan, the Iron Age vitrified fort does not seem to have been redefended, but inside the ramparts excavation revealed an occupation level with several hearths and one clay-floored hut, dated by radio-carbon to around AD 370. Associated finds included a clay mould for casting an escutcheon for a hanging bowl, a spindle whorl, whetstones and a palette.

Two other fortified sites have been excavated in Pictland. The first is Clatchard Craig in Fife. This had several periods of occupation, starting in the neolithic. Radio-carbon dating suggested that the defences of the fort were the work of the sixth or seventh centuries, and these were associated with imported Mediterranean pottery, moulds for making brooches and pins, a glass bead and piece of vessel glass, a silver ingot, and an assortment of iron and bone objects and pieces of shale bracelets. There were some finds of an earlier date from the fort, including some Roman Samian pottery and an openwork ornament, suggesting that, prior to the building of the ramparts, the site was occupied around the second or third centuries AD. Structural evidence for buildings inside the fort was minimal.

The most impressive of the Pictish forts that have been excavated is perhaps Dundurn in Perthshire. Dundurn is mentioned twice in documentary sources, first as Dun Duirn, in a reference in the Annals of Ulster to a siege there in 683; the other in a reference in the Scottish regnal lists to the death there in AD 889 of Girg, son of Dungal.

In its final phase, Dundurn comprised a roughly oval citadel with a high terrace and four lower terraces enclosed by ramparts, with an earthen enclosure and processional way on the north-west. A further enclosure has been noted to the north-east. This layout was achieved after a series of structural developments. First the upper terrace was enclosed with a timber palisade which radio-carbon dating suggested had been put up in the period AD 460–645. The palisade was subsequently dismantled, and replaced by a timber and stone wall. The timbering comprised beams and planks, nailed at right angles to one

Figure 64 Silver mount for a blast horn. This is among the few surviving finds from Burghead. It is decorated in the Anglo-Saxon 'Trewhiddle' style, named after a hoard from Cornwall deposited in the ninth century, and has animals in voids. (Photo: Trustees of the British Museum)

Figure 65 Dundurn, Perthshire. This is one of the best-documented Pictish forts, recorded as having been besieged in 683. Excavations carried out in 1976–7 by Professor Leslie Alcock established that the citadel had a timber-laced rampart and that the site was exclusively early medieval. (Photo: David Longley)

another and possibly filled with wickerwork. These were laid horizontally between layers of sand and rubble. Nails were used to fasten the timbers, and the overall character was similar to that of the timber lacing at Burghead. The front of the rampart rested on horizontal beams, set in rock-cut grooves, and the back of the rampart was tied to slots cut into the rock on the summit. Originally it was about 3.5–4.0 m wide and at least 2 m high. Belonging to this phase was extensive evidence for

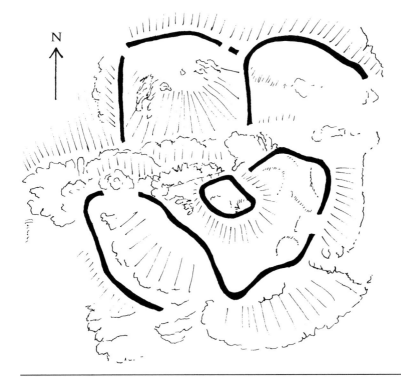

N

Figure 66 Plan of Dundurn. Width: 200 m. (Drawing: Amanda Straw, after Alcock)

settlement on the upper terrace, including a wattle floor and a stone water tank, but excavation did not extend to the interior of the fort so little is known about internal buildings. This phase has been assigned to the beginning of the seventh century AD.

The timber-laced rampart was fired but new defences were built on top of the ruins, with a rubble rampart which probably followed the line of the original wall. Some timber may have been employed in its construction, which has been linked with the reported siege and is therefore dated to the late seventh century. Probably associated with this phase were the remains of a sandstone building which seems to have re-used mortared stones from a ruined Roman fort nearby. Below the citadel a massive rubble rampart was constructed, seemingly without timbering. The final constructional phase at Dundurn was marked by minor reinforcement of the terrace rampart.

Dundurn in its final phase is typical of a group of monuments termed 'nuclear forts'. These have an inner citadel and a series of out-works comprising sections of rampart, often joined to natural outcrops to produce a series of subsidiary enclosures. The classic site is Dalmahoy in British-held territory in Midlothian, but Dunadd in Argyll is also of this type.

There is growing evidence that such nuclear forts were a phenome-non of the early Middle Ages. It is quite clear that those of Dundurn and Dunadd were not defensive works pre-dating the sixth or seventh centuries AD. In other cases, earlier Iron Age defences, for example at Clatchard Craig, may have been assimilated into the Dark Age defen-sive scheme. What is fundamental to most if not all of these forts is the choice of craggy hills, which enabled the defences to be organized with a central stronghold or citadel within a wider series of enclosures. Related to the nuclear forts of the type represented by Dundurn are other types of defensive enclosures found in Dark Age Britain and Ireland. Here a similar arrangement of central enclosure and outworks can be discerned. Typical of such sites is Cahercommaun in County Clare, with a stone-walled rath or ringfort set within a less substantial outer enclosure divided up by partition walls. In North Wales, Dinas Emrys is generally similar. As such, they reflect a social organization and hierarchy in Dark Age Britain in which the chiefs or kings presided from their citadels over their followers. Instead of the large tribal groupings of people represented by the hillforts in Iron Age Britain, these were probably much smaller social groups. Within the fort and its outworks, food supplies could have been stored and industrial activities carried out, while beyond in the surrounding countryside the mass of the subject population continued their farming lifestyle.

The forts of Dark Age Scotland (and, for that matter, the rest of Britain) do not seem to have outlived the ninth century. There is some evidence of activity at Burghead in the time of the Vikings, and a simi-lar story can be told at Dunadd or Dumbarton Rock, the stronghold of the Strathclyde Britons. Thereafter, as far as can be judged, the centres of power in Pictland shifted once again to low-lying courts not unlike the palaces occupied by later Saxon kings at such centres as Cheddar, Somerset. These later power centres of Pictland comprise sites such as Forteviot, Scone, Abernethy (see p. 27) and St Andrews.

These later centres are strongly linked to ecclesiastical foci: St Andrews was one of the most important religious centres in early medieval Scotland; at Abernethy a fine Irish-style round tower survives; Scone was where the later kings of the Scots were crowned; and Forteviot is notable for being mentioned in documentary sources as having a *palacium* (palace or royal hall) in the time of Kenneth mac Alpin. Although traditions relating to a palace on a site called Haly Hill at Forteviot were believed in the nineteenth century, the evidence is not very conclusive. Crop marks detected by aerial photography, however, have shown that south-east of the present village there lay a series of prehistoric and later ritual monuments, of which the latest identified are rectangular Pictish burial enclosures. Also from Forteviot has come the fine sculptured stone arch which clearly adorned a substantial building, presumably a royal church in which it would probably have served as an internal archway.

It must not be thought, however, that all the remains of settlement in Pictland in the historical period relate to forts and royal centres. Aerial photographic surveys of southern Pictland have revealed significant complexes of monuments. Scattered through Strathmore, on the banks of the Tay near Scone, around Inverness, in upper Strathearn and north-east Fife, as well as elsewhere in north-east Scotland, have been identified what appear to be rectangular timber buildings ('halls'). The discovery that one apparently 'Dark Age' hall at Balbridie in Aberdeenshire was in fact Neolithic suggests extreme caution should be exercised in identifying all these sites as Dark Age, but in a few cases there are other clues which point to a medieval rather than prehistoric date. At Lathrisk in Fife, no fewer than five buildings of this type are clustered together. Each has an annex at one end, generally similar to that detected in the Dark Age hall at Doon Hill, Dunbar, in East Lothian. Although, as has been seen, souterrains appear to have been demolished by around AD 200, one site, Pitroddie near Perth, has five separate souterrains along with ring-ditches and barrows. The site is overlooked by a multi-rampart hillfort. The name is, of course, a Pit- place-name, perhaps suggesting continuity of the site into the early medieval period.

In Atlantic Scotland, occupation continued on broch sites until the arrival of the Vikings. In Orkney, brochs themselves continued to be occupied into the third or even fourth century AD. In Shetland, however, by the early second century, they were being supplanted by 'wheelhouses' – round stone huts with radial piers – and similar structures appeared in the Hebrides. In Orkney, the wheelhouse never became popular; instead, figure-of-eight houses seem to have become fashionable. Similar buildings are also found in some parts of the Hebrides where they replaced earlier wheelhouses, for example at the

Udal, North Uist, where they made their appearance between AD 200 and 400, accompanied by a new artefact assemblage.

Of the Orcadian houses the best excavated is perhaps at Buckquoy, on the mainland opposite the tidal island of Birsay. There was a series of superimposed buildings on the site, spanning the period from the seventh to the ninth centuries – the last phase was Norse. Of the Pictish phase there were three major buildings, constructed with upright slabs and drystone walling. The first house was relatively simple with a series of sub-rectangular cells. Its replacement was a trefoil-shaped house. The third building in the sequence, which was dated to the eighth century, was far more substantial (four-and-a-half times the size of its predecessor). It had three rooms with an entrance vestibule, approached via two entrances, one a paved path into the main living hall, the other leading via a vestibule into an ante-chamber. Around the central hearth was a kerb, presumably to take wooden benches. At least part of the building seems to have had a hipped roof, though a partly subterranean room off the main hall probably used for storage may have had a corbelled roof.

The precise plan of the Buckquoy house is without parallel, but buildings of a similar shape have been recognized at the Udal and at Yarrows, Caithness, while related structures occur on some broch sites, such as Nybster, also in Caithness.

Settlement and Economy in Iron Age Argyll

In the early Iron Age, Argyll lay at the extremity of the Atlantic province, and the dominant feature of the landscape was a network of small, stone-walled forts (duns). All but one excavated example (Rahoy) seem, from associated finds, to date no earlier than the first or second centuries AD. Many seem to have continued in use, and may still have been constructed, in the time of the historic kingdom of Dalriada.

The limited amount of excavation that has been done suggests that duns and larger forts were first built and occupied in the first millennium BC. Dunagoil on Bute was a large fort, occupied from the late Bronze Age through to c. AD 1000. On a couple of sites, Dun Skeig in Kintyre, and Dun Mac Sniachan in Lorn, larger forts seem to have been replaced by smaller duns on the same site.

For the most part, the duns of Argyll appear to have been simple fortified farmsteads enclosed by a single drystone wall, with a single entrance and without outlying ditches. Each dun seems to have been the home of a single family unit, in contrast to the earlier forts. These latter enclosed, within the encircling stone rampart, a diversity of stone-walled round houses, and presumably served as the centres of Iron Age chiefs of varying status. The smaller forts were perhaps the strongholds of sub-kings.

There has been some debate about whether the duns contained

Figure 67 Buckquoy, near Birsay, Orkney, after excavation by Dr Anna Ritchie. This site had a succession of Pictish- and Viking-period building phases. The Pictish house seen here is typical of a category of figure-of-eight buildings found in Orkney and the Hebrides. (Photo: Scottish Development Department)

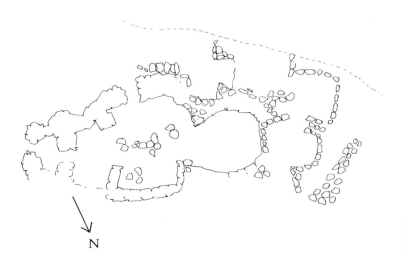

N

Figure 68 Plan of the Pictish house at Buckquoy, Orkney. Width: 150 m. (Drawing: Amanda Straw, after Ritchie)

Figure 69 Stone-walled fort or dun, Ardifuir, Argyll. Originally occupied in the first or second century AD, finds of ingot moulds and a crucible suggest this was also occupied in the time of the Scots. (Photo: David Longley)

separate, stone-built huts or whether they were totally roofed. While the larger, irregularly shaped duns would have been impossible to roof and must have enclosed separate buildings (as appears to have been the case with the sub-triangular dun at Kildonan), as many fifty per cent or even more of the Argyll duns may have been totally roofed. Many have an internal diameter of less than 15 m.

Outside the forts were sometimes located enclosures which may have been used for various industrial purposes. In a few cases it has been possible to discern evidence for early agriculture. It is quite clear that one's view of what was adequate agricultural land is coloured by modern concepts of farming. Terraces and field-walls have been found

Figure 70 Detail of the walling in the dun at Ardifuir, Argyll. Its building techniques share features with the Atlantic brochs, including intra-mural chambers. (Photo: David Longley)

adjacent to duns and, though these cannot be proved to be contemporary, they seem to relate to the duns rather than later farming activity. In the same way, the crannogs seem to be positioned in relation to potential farmland nearby.

The duns and crannogs of Argyll hardly represent a total population of the region in the Iron Age. A notable feature of the excavated sites has been the presence of Roman material – pieces of pottery and glass, and sometimes bronzes. Elsewhere in Scotland, as has been seen, the presence of Roman material on native sites is an indication of their high status; in Ireland, crannogs were the homes of people of high rank. Dr Margaret Nieke has suggested that the fortified sites of Argyll should be seen as the high-ranking homes of the élite, and that society in Iron Age Argyll depended, as it did elsewhere in the Celtic world, on a network of client relationships, with the exchange of agricultural products and services in return for protection and other support. Welsh laws of the early Middle Ages suggest that this applied to kings only, but it is clear that in early historic Ireland the term 'king' applied to a diversity of ranks in a pyramid with 'high kings' at the top, and it is likely that clientage operated on a number of levels in Iron Age Argyll.

According to the Roman-period geographer Ptolemy, writing in the second century AD, the tribe in this area, noted for horse-rearing, was known as the Epidii. Although animal bones from excavations do not include a particularly high proportion of horse remains, Adomnan's Life of Columba shows that horses were important to the early Christian community on Iona in the seventh century. Cattle, pigs, sheep and goats figure in the remains recovered from the broch at Dun Mor Vaul on Tiree, occupied from the first to third centuries AD.

Forts and Farms in Dalriada

The arrival of the Scots does not seem to have brought about any major change in the settlement pattern or types of Argyll. Relatively little excavation has been carried out on sites occupied in this period, but there is evidence that some duns at least were occupied or reoccupied at periods up to the coming of the Vikings. Similarly, crannogs continued to be built and occupied.

One novel feature in Dark Age Dalriada, however, was the occupation of rocky citadels. Documentary sources allude to four such strongholds in the region, Dunollie (Dun Ollaigh), Dunadd, Tairpirt Boittir and Aberte. Of these nothing is known about the identity of Tairpirt Boittir. Aberte has been identified as Dunaverty, at the tip of Kintyre. This is an impressive rock stack, now without any visible evidence of early medieval occupation. It has not been excavated, but is known (if the identification is correct) to have been besieged in 712.

Both Dunollie and Dunadd have been excavated, though the former very selectively. Dunollie today is a precipitous and rocky promontory

Figure 71 Dunollie, Argyll, from the sea. This site is now dominated by a medieval castle, but excavation by Professor Leslie Alcock confirmed that it was occupied by the Scots around the seventh century and was defended by a rampart. (Photo: David Longley)

standing above Oban Bay, on which the dominant feature is a medieval castle. The site, however, is the most prominently figured in the Irish *Annals* – it is mentioned in five entries between 686 and 734. The entry for 701 refers to its destruction, while that for 714 to its (re)building by Selbach of the Cenel Loairn. Excavation showed that the earliest occupation of the site was possibly unfortified, and was marked by the presence, among others, of a bronzesmith who fashioned pins. An iron spearhead and arrowtips point additionally to a more military presence. This first phase at Dunollie has been dated to the period between the seventh and ninth centuries AD, and presumably was the occupation destroyed by Selbach. The finds of metalwork and imported pottery suggest that the first Dalriadic occupation was by a person of some importance (confirmed by its sack warranting mention in the Irish Annals), and perhaps there was a dun on the site destroyed by the later castle, as its excavator, Leslie Alcock, has suggested.

The rebuilding involved a more extensive programme of fortification. A rubble bank revetted with massive slabs and with a rear kerb was constructed, 5 m wide where the ground sloped away less steeply, 2 m wide where it fronted a precipitous drop. Although it cannot be proved, this rampart may represent the rebuilding by Selbach. The rampart became reduced and grassed over, but occupation continued until the tenth century.

The finds from Dunollie were very varied and included imported pottery of Class E, a composite decorated antler comb, a T-shaped woodman's axe, a hammerhead, a glass bead, a loop of gold wire and a piece of a rim of a painted Roman glass vessel. The latter might have been an 'heirloom', a gift perhaps as part of a Roman buy-off in the time of the first settlements in Dalriada. Two pieces of very coarse pottery may have been locally made.

About Dunadd there is more information, since it was extensively excavated early in the twentieth century (1904 and 1929) and again in

Figure 72 Dunadd, Argyll, the most famous fort occupied by the Scots and generally believed to have been their capital. Excavated on two occasions before the Second World War and again in 1980–1, it has produced a wealth of finds from the early medieval period. (Photo: Scottish Development Department)

1980–81. Dunadd is a rocky outcrop in the Crinan Moss of mid-Argyll, located between Loch Fyne and the Sound of Jura, which in Dalriadic times was defended by the surrounding marshlands. Traditionally, Dunadd has been seen as the capital of the Dalriadic Scots, but there is no real evidence for this. It only figures in documentary sources twice, once when it was besieged in 683 (*obsessio Duin Att:* 'siege of Dunadd'), and once in 736 when 'Angus, Fergus' son, king of the

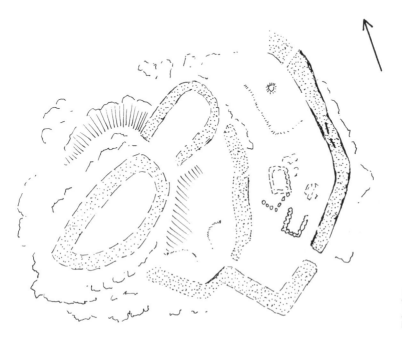

Figure 73 Plan of Dunadd. Width: 120 m. (Drawing: Amanda Straw, after Craw and Lane)

Picts, wasted the districts of Dalriada, gained Dunadd, and burned Creic; and he bound with chains two sons of Selbach, namely Dungal and Feradach'. Claims have been made that prior to the settlement of Dalriada by Fergus, Dunadd was a fortress held by the Picts in Pictish territory. Although there are a few finds from Dunadd that pre-date AD 500, there is nothing that suggests there was any fortification on the site before the settlement of Dalriada. There is no evidence either that the area was held by Picts, though it is inherently likely that much of Scotland north of the Forth–Clyde line was Pictish in the fifth century.

One feature of Dunadd which has taxed commentators is the series of carvings on a rock-face just below the summit fort. It comprises an incised carving of a boar, an ogham inscription, a basin or hollow, and a deeply carved outline of a human foot, with a more lightly carved human foot adjacent. The 'basin' may be a Bronze Age cup mark, but what about the others? The most popularly expressed explanation is that the boar and ogham inscriptions were carved by victorious Picts, perhaps on their capture of the site in 736.

There are four reasons why this is unlikely. First, why did the Scots when they reoccupied the site (as they did into the ninth century) not destroy the marks of their defeat? Second, as far as is known, the Picts were not carving incised symbols as late as the second quarter of the eighth century; by this time, relief-carved symbols on cross-slabs were the norm (see p. 104). Third, the boar is without any precise counterpart in Pictland – it only looks Pictish because it is naturalistic. Finally, there are no other Pictish symbols in Dalriada. There are, however, other fairly naturalistic animal representations. For example, incised on a motif-piece which came from the summit fort during the 1980–1 excavations, is a stag, as well as interlace patterns that some have seen as

Figure 74 Entrance to the fort, Dunadd, Argyll. (Photo: David Longley)

Figure 75 Carvings on a rock-face at Dunadd. The boar has been interpreted as a Pictish carving, executed after a victorious campaign in Dalriada, but this seems unlikely. The foot-shaped indentation, it has been suggested, was used in the inauguration of Scottish kings. (Photos: David Longley, L. Laing)

late medieval. But as the excavator, Alan Lane, has pointed out, there is no reason why a late medieval motif piece should turn up on this, by now abandoned, site. The boar could just as easily be Scottish as Pictish, or, if it is Pictish, could have been carved in the fifth century before Dalriadic occupation.

Nor need the ogham inscription be Pictish. It seems likely that ogham was acquired by the Picts from the Scots of Dalriada. The Dunadd inscription has features that show it to be related to Irish ogham and to be earlier than the main series of Pictish inscriptions – the date most recently suggested for it is in the seventh century. If that is the case, despite its blundered meaning it could as easily be Dalriadic as Pictish.

The remaining carvings, of human footprints, are thought by some to have been intended for the inauguration of Scottic kings, who would have placed one foot in the carving during the ceremony. Alan Lane has suggested that all the carvings relate to a Scottic inauguration ceremony, and the Pictish flavour might be accounted for by a suggestion of Pictish overlordship. This would not explain, however, the presence of a similar footprint on the Iron Age fort and broch site at Clickhimin in Shetland.

The defences of Dunadd are complex and reveal a varied history. Two main phases of construction have been recognized in the summit fort, but the relationship of this to the other forts or enclosures below the summit is not clear. The summit fort is enclosed by a stone wall defining an inner citadel, with other stone walls flanking it at a lower level. The lower flat top of the hill is encircled by a substantial drystone wall, to which entrance was gained through a narrow passageway, presumably blocked by a wooden gateway. There are platforms, terraces and portions of walling that relate to various buildings which must have stood within the enclosure. The summit fort's wall was about 4 m wide, and still stands about 1 m high. It was built on top of an earlier fortification on a different alignment.

Figure 76 Some finds from Dunadd, Argyll. (a) Viking period trial-piece, (b) stone with a Christian inscription in Irish lettering (I(N)NOMINE (DEI): 'In the name of God'), perhaps used as a grave marker, (c) composite bone comb, and (d) Viking trial-piece. Dimensions: 9.6 cm, 7.7 cm, 4.5 cm, 6.7 cm. (Drawing: Amanda Straw)

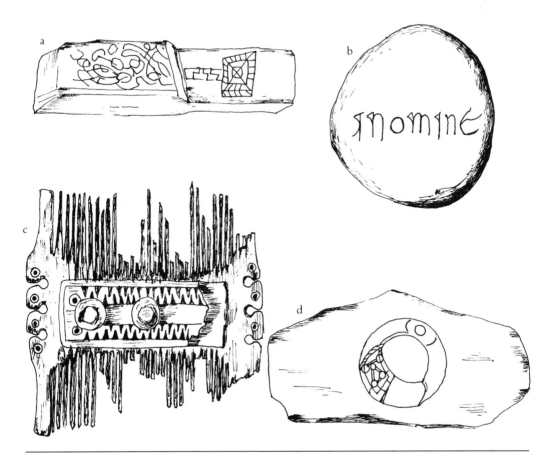

The finds from Dunadd are rich, compatible with a site of high status. They include evidence for ornamental metalwork, (extending perhaps from the seventh into the eighth or ninth centuries), ironwork and a variety of other activities. A large number of rotary querns showed that corn was ground on the site, perhaps for redistribution to the surrounding area. Plant remains included wheat, barley, oats and hazelnuts. Imported pottery included both D and E Ware from France. Dunadd has produced more E Ware than any other site in Britain, suggesting it may have been a distributive centre. The ironwork is rich and varied and includes weapons as well as more mundane artefacts. One or two were purely Irish in character, such as an iron-hafted saw and an iron object of uncertain function with a broad, slotted head. Lignite (or jet?) was made into bracelets and there was a variety of glass beads. Among the unusual finds was an Anglo-Saxon bronze mount, and a gold and garnet stud from an Anglo-Saxon brooch of the seventh century; a motif-piece with a design for a Viking Age brooch (showing the continuing occupation of the site); and an enamelled roundel with interlace betraying Anglo-Saxon connections. A cross-inscribed quern stone from the site appears to have been carved by a monk from Iona – it has a type of cross concentrated in Argyll which is derived from the monastery at Iona, implying a link between the two places. The finds from Dunadd include a piece of the mineral orpiment, used to make the brilliant yellow colour employed in manuscripts. This was obtained in Classical times from Italy and Turkey and is particularly significant since it was used in the Book of Kells, probably made on Iona (see p. 155). Further evidence for a Christian presence at Dunadd is implied by a stone with an inscription, 'INOMINE [DEI]': 'In the name of God', datable to around the eighth century. Adomnan reported that Columba visited the 'caput regionis' (chief centre of the region) which has been taken as meaning Dunadd. Here he apparently met Gaulish merchants, which would be supported by the fact that the Dunadd E Ware came from Gaul.

The fortified citadels of Dalriada were clearly linked with outlying smaller farmsteads, most notably the duns and crannogs. A number of duns were occupied within the Dalriadic period: Kildonan, Kidalloig, Dun Fhinn, Duin an Fheurain, An Caisteal, Leccamore, Dun Eilean Righ I, Ugadale Point, and Ardifuir. All of these have produced finds of this period.

It is probably reasonable to regard the duns as the seats of men of varying social standing who were subject to the overlordship of the rulers in the four great strongholds. Below these there would of course have been other farmers of lesser status, who in turn came under the authority of the dun occupiers. The duns of the early Christian period may have been the Dalriadic Scottish equivalent of the raths of Ireland.

Documentary evidence makes it clear that the social organization of Dalriada centred on the king and his tribe (*tuath*) and, above them, overkings who could assert control over three kindreds or more. The Senchus fer nAlban provides a list of the holdings (*tech*) of the free farmers in Dalriada. A survey of Islay shows that there are far more households listed in the Senchus than there are surviving duns.

The remaining type of site known to have been occupied in Dark Age Argyll is the crannog. A single example, at Loch Glashan, has yielded a variety of finds of this period, including a fine bronze brooch of a type current in Pictland, and the leatherwork and woodwork mentioned earlier (p. 68).

CHAPTER 4

Art of the Picts and the Scots

Both the Picts and the Scots had a flourishing art. Indeed, the most enduring legacy that the Picts have left for later generations is their art. The Scots were less prolific – apart from a few notable sculptures there are few works that can be categorically assigned to them. However there is a good reason to believe that three of the most outstanding works of Dark Age Celtic art, the Book of Durrow, the Book of Kells and the Hunterston Brooch, were at least partly the product of the Irish in western Scotland.

The Study of Pictish Art

The art of the Picts fascinated antiquaries as long ago as the eighteenth century, when major sculptures were drawn and illustrated as attractions to be visited by enthusiastic travellers in northern Scotland. By the early nineteenth century, speculation had begun on the meaning of the mysterious symbols that appeared on many of these stones. But it was not until the end of the century that a real attempt was made to collect, illustrate and analyse the surviving examples of Pictish sculpture. Originally the Society of Antiquaries of Scotland proposed to employ (at the cost of £100) a researcher to visit and describe the monuments, and to call upon the leading expert of the day, Joseph Anderson, to interpret them in a series of lectures to be delivered in 1892. The person who undertook the daunting task of preparing the catalogue was Romilly Allen, already experienced from his studies of sculptures in Wales. In 1903 Allen and Anderson put the results of their work together in a massive volume, *The Early Christian Monuments of Scotland,* which is still an indispensible starting point for anyone studying Pictish art today.

Allen and Anderson prosaically divided the sculptures of Pictland into three groups. Class I comprised slabs of undressed stone with symbols incised on them. Class II were dressed slabs with a Christian cross as the main element of their decoration, but with Pictish symbols and other subjects also depicted. These monuments were carved in relief. The third group, Class III, comprised similar examples of relief carving, but lacked the Pictish symbols.

Allen and Anderson saw the three classes as being in chronological sequence. Class I they believed to date from the sixth and seventh centuries, Class II from the eighth to ninth centuries, and Class III from the ninth century and later. Although their classification has much to recommend it, like many such simple schemes it has produced a straightjacket that has hampered positive thought on the dating of the stones. There is, for example, no real reason to assume that Class I stones did not continue to be made at the same time as Class II monuments in some areas, nor any evidence that Class II stones suddenly stopped being erected around 843, the time of the amalgamation of Picts and Scots under Kenneth mac Alpin, as Allen and Anderson believed, nor that all Class III stones post-date 843.

The Mystery of the Pictish Symbols

Any study of Pictish art begins with the symbols. These have become central to all discussions of the Picts and, by virtue of their ability to perplex scholars, are probably inflated in importance beyond what is reasonable. There are about forty to fifty different symbols, not only incised on stone slabs, but also found on cave walls and on small portable objects of stone, bone, bronze and silver.

Even a cursory glance at the repertoire of Pictish symbols reveals that they fall into two main groups: representations of animals, either real or, very occasionally, mythical; and abstract designs, of which some seem to be representations of objects, for example a mirror or comb, and others appear simply to be patterns.

A closer survey of the 160 or so symbol stones from Scotland shows that the symbols rarely appear singly, more commonly occurring in combinations of two to four. They do not overlap and seldom touch, and most frequently are in pairs with an animal element combined with an 'abstract' element. When the distribution of particular symbols is mapped, it becomes apparent that there is no obvious regional distribution of any one type. This suggests that the symbols are not related to particular territories within Pictland but were understood throughout the lands in which they are found.

There are several related problems posed by the symbols and the stones on which they are found. What is the date of the symbols? Were they devised at one point in time, or were they created over a long period? Were they in existence in other media before they were incised on stone? When were they carved on stone and over what period? What do the symbols mean (if anything), both individually and in combination? What was the purpose of the stones, and why were the symbols also marked on objects and rock surfaces?

Figure 77 Repaired Pictish symbol stone from Brandsbutt, Aberdeenshire. This has an ogham inscription added, perhaps from the eighth century (the carving is deeper than that used on the symbols). (Photo: Jim Henderson)

The most widely held view is that the symbol stones and the symbols carved on them came into being in the seventh century AD. It has been argued that certain of the animal symbols are very close to evangelist symbols that appear in early Insular manuscripts, most notably the Book of Durrow and the Echternach Gospels, where, for example, the same kind of treatment of shoulder and hip spirals can be found, and where the heads of the animals are segmented off from the neck. In particular, the lion in the Book of Durrow has been compared with Pictish beasts which have similar, truncated snouts. While nobody would deny the similarities, it has to be said that the device of hip and shoulder spirals can be found both earlier than the time of the Book of Durrow (on the fifth-century BC flagons from Basse-Yutz in Celtic Gaul, for example), and much later (for instance in Viking art). Futher, only the eagle, the salmon and the bull (calf) appear in both Pictish sculpture and Insular manuscripts, while the Picts have a range of creatures peculiar to their own tradition. Study of the Pictish creatures, too,

Figure 78 (opposite) An assortment of Pictish symbols. (Drawing: L. Laing, after Henderson)

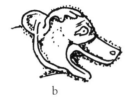

Figure 79 Comparison of Pictish symbols and animals in Insular Gospel books. (a) Book of Durrow, lion, (b) Meigle, stone 26, (c) Echternach Gospels, calf, (d) Dores, fragmentary boar carving

shows them to have been far more accomplished and confident than their manuscript counterparts, and if any copying were involved, the manuscript scribes probably copied Pictish beasts, rather than vice versa. When all the Pictish symbols are considered (not just the animals), and the designs broken down into their component parts, it becomes apparent that the artistic repertoire of the Picts was different from and simpler than that of the manuscript illuminator. For example, absent in Pictish symbol art are the complex spiral and interlace patterns of the Book of Durrow. To explain this by pointing to the difficulties of translating Durrow-type patterns to stone is insufficient, since later Celtic artists had no problems in translating extremely complex designs, including those that appear in Insular manuscripts, into relief carving.

Those who argue in favour of a seventh-century invention of the Pictish symbols also raise another problem. If it is accepted that the symbols were being carved in relief on Class II stones by the end of the seventh century (as other evidence might suggest), it implies that Class I stones were put up over an incredibly short period of time, perhaps twenty-five or fifty years, unless they continued to be carved into the eighth century alongside the Class II monuments.

It has to be emphasized that the Class I–III system devised by Allen and Anderson is in many ways misleading, since the supposed

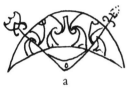

a

b

c

d

e

f

Figure 80 The 'declining' Pictish symbols: a suggestion of how some symbols degenerated from their original form. (Drawing: L. Laing, after Stevenson and Henderson)

chronological sequence of the stones by extension has come to be applied to the dating of the different symbols, which is a separate issue. Normally the method employed would be to take a date before which (*terminus ante quem*) and a date after which (*terminus post quem*) each symbol is not found, and then analyse the result. But few if any of the symbols are certainly more than reminiscent of any datable material.

One theory that has attracted a number of commentators is that of the 'declining' symbol. This school of thought points to the fact that symbols on Class I stones are remarkably uniform, but that the same symbols are rendered in variant forms on Class II stones. If this theory is correct (this issue is considered further below, p. 111), then thirty-five to fifty years again seems a remarkably short period in which the symbols could have 'declined' from their original forms.

Another case advanced by the supporters of a seventh-century invention of the symbols rests in the general absence of symbols from Dalriada. According to this view they must post-date the Dalriadic colonization of *c.* 500. This, of course, only makes them later than the fifth century, and would not exclude their use in the sixth. In any event, however, the distribution of Class I symbol stones is, except for five examples in the Hebrides, exclusively confined to eastern and northern Scotland, and it can be argued that whenever the symbols were first used, their usage on the stones had not spread sufficiently westwards before the sixth century.

It has also been suggested that the symbol stones must post-date the conversion of the Picts to Christianity, since the symbols appear with Christian crosses and other Christian subject matter on the Class II stones. This is however, invalid as a clue to the date of the stones. First, even if the symbols were devised by the pagan Picts, they may not have had a specifically pagan meaning (and indeed, most interpretations of them have favoured a secular explanation). Second, even if they were pagan, there is plenty of evidence for pagan subject matter being used on other Early Christian stones (crosses of the Viking Age often have scenes from pagan Scandinavian mythology; and nearer the time of the Pictish symbols, the eighth-century Northumbrian Franks casket has the Adoration of the Magi next to an episode from the legend of Wayland Smith).

Of course, even though the arguments supporting a seventh-century invention of the Pictish symbols do not stand up to scrutiny, it does not mean that Pictish symbols could not have been incised on stone in the seventh or even the eighth century.

Is it possible to date any of the symbols to before the seventh century? At Pool, on Sanday in the Orkneys, sixth-century alterations to the structures involved re-use of two stones as component elements: one carried an inscription in the ogham alphabet, the other a crude double-disc and serpent head, combined with a third symbol somewhat like a crescent moon. The excavator, Dr John Hunter, suggested that the slab had been laid face-down deliberately, and that the symbols on it should be classed as 'proto-symbols' on account of their crudity. These are comparable with the engravings on the cave walls at East Wemyss, Fife. The sixth-century date is supported by radio-carbon dating, and, as the stone was seemingly re-used, it could be much earlier.

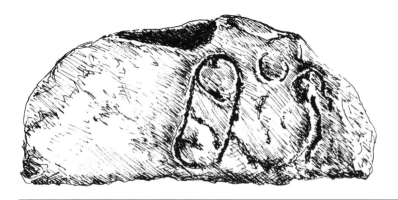

Figure 81 Symbol stone with 'proto-symbol' of double-disc, Pool, Sanday, Orkney. Width: 32 cm. (Drawing: Amanda Straw)

The stone is not the only find of Pictish symbols from Pool: a bone object, shaped like a pin, bore a crude double-disc and Z-rod and part of a rectangular design. A radio-carbon date suggested that it might be as early as the fourth century AD. A further find of a cattle phalanx had a crescent and V-rod symbol along with other incised designs, and was datable to the fifth to seventh centuries AD. Dr Anna Ritchie has suggested that possible support for this early date takes the form of what may be a double-disc symbol engraved on a native silver version of a Roman crossbow brooch. This was found at Carn Liath, Caithness, in a settlement outside a broch. The brooch also has a pair of pelta patterns, in keeping with Pictish symbol art, and a pattern not unlike one found on silver in the Norrie's Law hoard (see below). Crossbow brooches in gold and silver were high-status objects that were generally worn by high-ranking Roman army officers. Could the model have been booty from a successful campaign against the Romans?

If it is accepted that proto-symbols were current before the fully evolved symbols came into use, then the symbols carved on cave walls assume a special prominence, since for the most part they are much more crudely carved than those on the slabs. A major collection can be seen on the walls of the Sculptor's Cave, Covesea, Moray, in the heart of Pictland. The Covesea cave was occupied in the late Bronze Age, and again in the period of the Roman occupation of Britain. Excavation of the cave floor produced an astonishing array of Romano-British artefacts, most notably pins, nail cleaners and tweezers In addition, there was a series of forty-two Roman bronze coins, mostly barbarous British imitations but nine official issues of the period AD 337–354, of which three were totally unworn and three pierced.

Figure 82 Proto-symbols carved on the walls of the Sculptor's cave, Covesea, Moray. (L. Laing, after Diack)

The excavator, Miss Sylvia Benton, thought that there were two periods of occupation in the Sculptor's Cave during the currency of the Roman artefacts, one in the second century and one in the fourth. Although the finds included some pieces of second-century Roman Samian pottery, such material is known from elsewhere to have survived even into the fifth and sixth centuries, and the remaining finds are not particularly diagnostic of a second-century date. In any event, not a single find later than the fourth century came to light in the excavations, and it was concluded that the carvings on the cave walls were contemporary with the Roman period occupation. Miss Benton suggested that the occupation was not domestic: 'I do feel rather strongly that none of these articles [the Roman finds] are really suitable for cave-dwellers. Perhaps I am prejudiced by the extreme difficulty we had in detecting the bronzes. We kept losing excavation knives and entrenching tools. How could those people have kept nail-cleaners and tweezers, and who would have the heart to clean nails in the Sculptor's Cave?' (Benton, 'Excavation of the Sculptor's Cave, Covesea', *Proceedings of the Society of Antiquaries of Scotland* (1931), p. 205). She also pointed to the numerous human bones (and a wisp of red human hair) from the cave floor, and the fact that there were no fewer than nine beheadings attested by the bones.

The finds from the Sculptor's Cave are all in keeping with its use in the fourth century for rituals, perhaps connected with a shrine. Roman toilet articles and coins are uncommon in Scotland after the second century AD, and the concentration in the Sculptor's Cave is compatible with its ritual use. So too are the bodies which may have been those of sacrificial victims. In 739 the Pictish king, Talorgen, was drowned by his overlord Oengus. This has been seen by some to represent a survival of pagan ritual sacrifice, which is also attested in early Christian Ireland.

Figure 83 East Wemyss caves. Pictish and later engravings are carved on the walls. (Photo: David Longley)

Figure 84 Symbols carved on the walls of Jonathan's cave, East Wemyss, Fife. (Photos: David Longley)

Similar carvings have been found on the cave walls at East Wemyss, Fife, but here the caves were used in subsequent periods and the carvings, which include at least one of a later date, could have been made at any time.

A survey of the symbols themselves can also provide some clues as to their date. They may well have been devised over a period of time. Professor Charles Thomas suggested that many of the abstract symbols were representations of objects of the pre-Roman Iron Age, and that the symbols originated as tattoos on the bodies of Picts. The suggestion that the symbols may have been tattoos is a strong one: they are clearly devised as drawn, two-dimensional designs, and would have posed problems for Pictish artists when they were translated into relief on the Class II stones.

A few of the symbols might date back to the later Iron Age, as Professor Thomas suggested. For example, a 'sword' symbol (usually termed a 'tuning fork') found on a stone from Dunrobin, Sutherland, has a type of hilt-guard that can be matched in a surviving example from Castlehill, Dalry, Ayrshire, found with Roman material of the second century, and with a sword from Cotterdale in the North Riding of Yorkshire. Both belong to a group of Brigantian swords found in northern England and southern Scotland. As

Professor Thomas has noted, an even closer parallel for the Dunrobin sword can be seen in a surviving sword from Hod Hill, Dorset, an outlier of the Brigantian group. He has also argued that the spears shown in Pictish symbols have knobbed butts, again a type known in Scotland (and Ireland) in the later Iron Age. Moulds for making such spearbutts are known from Traprain Law, East Lothian, while Cassius Dio refers to their use by the Caledonians campaigning against Severus in the early third century. Two other symbols have been suggested as having Iron Age prototypes. The first is the double-disc, which looks similar to an opened-out massive armlet of the type current among the Caledonians. The last is a unique rendering of what has been seen as another piece of Caledonian metalwork, a 'Massive' or 'Donside' terret. All of the aforementioned objects are known to have been in use as late as the second century AD, and some, such as the Donside terrets, might have been current as late as the fourth.

Other symbols, however, seem to represent objects current later. The most informative are the symbols representing mirrors and combs. Two main types of comb are shown on the Pictish stones. One is a rectangular composite type with two sides of teeth and strengthening bars rivetted lengthwise across them. The second has a single line of teeth and an arched or more complex voluted back.

The simple composite comb has a long life, but does not appear to have been used much before the third or fourth century AD when it became fashionable in Roman Britain. Combs of this general type remained current until the Viking Age. A probable seventh-century example has been found in a lake dwelling at Buston in Ayrshire. All that can be inferred is that the symbol representing this type of comb is unlikely to pre-date the third or more probably the fourth century AD.

The single-sided combs with high backs that appear as symbols seem to have been current in the fourth and fifth centuries, and are found in both Ireland and Scotland. They are widespread in Atlantic Scotland, but surviving examples are difficult to date prior to the seventh century. One comb symbol does, however, seem to be more closely datable than the others, since the form of the symbol, albeit stylized, seems to suggest a type of Germanic comb current in the fifth century. Again, the surviving examples of similar combs in Scotland and Ireland are unlikely to pre-date the seventh century, but the prototypes must have arrived in the Celtic world at the time of their currency on the Continent. Of course, whether or not the symbols represent the original imports, or later Pictish versions, is impossible to say, owing to the stylization of the comb on the stones.

The mirror symbols have been compared with pre-Roman Iron Age mirrors. However, with the exception of one from south-west Scotland and one from County Mayo, such mirrors have not been found in northern Britain or Ireland, and other models can be found. A recent study of Roman mirrors has suggested that the models for Pictish mirror symbols should be sought in the Roman world.

When the designs are broken down into their component parts or 'grammar', it can readily be seen that the majority of decorative elements were those current in late Roman and early post-Roman Britain: pelta patterns, scrolls, trumpets, etc. Some of the abstract designs may have had a more direct inspiration in provincial Romano-British art. What looks like a double-disc, for example, appears on a Roman altar found at Chesterholm in Northumberland.

Mention was made earlier (p. 105) of the 'declining symbol'. Intensive study of the form of particular symbols has suggested that different symbols originated in different areas. This would fit in with the view, canvassed earlier, that the symbols were devised at various times, perhaps from the third or fourth century AD onwards, and originally used on perishable media (such as skin), but later being translated to stone and metal. There is no reason at present to date any of the stones earlier than the fifth century. At this time the idea of carving them on slabs may have been acquired by copying the memorial stones with Latin inscriptions that were being set up in southern Scotland, Wales and south-west England, themselves in imitation of Roman tombstones. This does not necessarily mean all symbol stones were tombstones, though it is possible that a good many were.

Figure 85 'Grammar' of Pictish symbol ornament. (Drawings: L. Laing)

Norrie's Law and Early Pictish Silverwork

One remarkable find sheds some light on the dating of the currency of the Pictish symbols. In the early years of the nineteenth century a hoard of silverwork came to light in a sandpit at Norrie's Law, Fife. The store was mostly composed of a variety of pieces from larger objects, seemingly folded and crushed as though for the melting pot, but included what at the time was described as a 'suit of armour' of silver, chain-mail, shield and helmet. Much of the find was unfortunately melted down, by a local jeweller, but a number of pieces were rescued, for example: two large penannular rings with expanded terminals; three pins of a type known as 'hand-pins'; two leaf-shaped plaques; a large silver roundel with a square cut out of it, which was clearly cut down from something larger, with two high relief bosses on it; a spoon bowl

Figure 86 Silver plaques with symbols, originally enamelled in red, from the hoard found at Norrie's Law, Fife, in the early nineteenth century. Height: 9 cm. (Photo: Royal Museums of Scotland)

bearing a Roman inscription; parts of spiral silver bracelets; finger rings; and some curiously decorated mounts. In addition there was a variety of pieces of silver scrap including some which appeared to be from late Roman plate, and a large roundel which may have been the covering for a circular shield. The hoard also contained two *siliquae* (silver coins) of the Roman emperors Valens and Constantius II (*c.* AD 337–378).

Some time after the hoard became widely known, a Miss Dundas, who clearly had indicated she would like to buy pieces from the find, was offered two bronze coins by a peddlar which he said had been found with the hoard. The first was a coin struck in the name of the daughter of Mark Antony and was of a type too early to have reached Britain with the Romans, let alone in the Dark Ages. The other was a Byzantine piece, probably of Justinian (AD 527–565) but wrongly identified as being of Tiberius Constantine (d. AD 682). Although Byzantine bronze coins are known from Britain, almost none have been authenticated as having arrived in the early Middle Ages. Students who have favoured a late date for Pictish symbols have assumed the Byzantine coin to be a genuine find and have followed its supposed date to assign the hoard to a deposition some time after 682. But the contemporary accounts state quite clearly that only silver was found at Norrie's Law, thus both bronze coins can be dismissed as spurious.

Where the importance of the hoard lies for the study of Pictish symbols is in the fact that the two leaf-shaped plaques and one of the hand-pins bear Pictish symbols.

The two hand-pins are virtually identical, except for the presence of a Z-rod on the back of one. It has been suggested, however, that one is a copy of the other, since the one with the symbol is less worn than that without. Both hand-pins have a pattern of stamped rings on the back which matches similar patterns on other silver hand-pins, one of which came from a late Roman context in a Roman site called Tripontium in Warwickshire. An earlier type of hand-pin was found with a hoard of Roman coins at Oldcroft in Gloucestershire, where it was believed the pin was an heirloom (it was very worn) when it was buried *c.* AD 360. The Oldcroft pin is simpler than the Tripontium pin, which in turn is stylistically slightly less evolved than the Norrie's Law pins, but there is no reason to suppose that the Norrie's Law and the Tripontium pins are widely separated in date.

Similar pins have also been found in Ireland and in another silver hoard from Pictland, discovered at Gaulcross in Banff, which, like that from Norrie's Law, mostly ended up in the melting pot. One pin, a chain and a bracelet were the only survivors. The Gaulcross bracelet, however, is closely comparable with fragments of bracelets in the Norrie's Law hoard, and as the pin has a similar pattern of rings on the back, both finds should be regarded as roughly contemporary. The Gaulcross hoard originally contained other pins and brooches. It was found shortly before 1840, buried in a Bronze Age ring cairn (stone circle).

The likeliest date for the Norrie's Law pins lies in the fifth century.

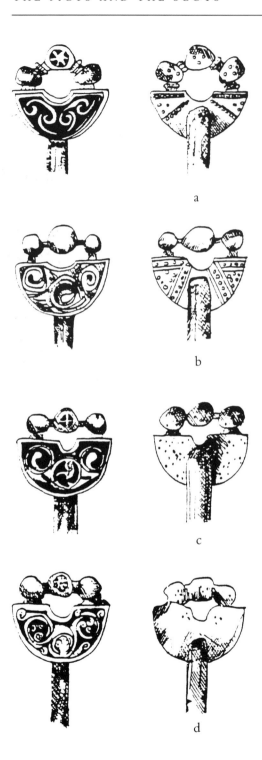

a

b

c

d

Figure 87 Silver handpins, all of related type with the same type of ring ornament on the back. They are from (a) the Roman site of Tripontium, Warwickshire, (b) Long Sutton, Somerset, (c) Norrie's Law, Fife and (d) the Gaulcross Hoard, Banff. (Drawing: L. Laing)

Figure 88 This silver brooch, found on a broch site at Carn Liath, Caithness, appears to be a copy of a Roman fourth-century crossbow brooch, the ornate silver and gold examples of which were worn by high ranking officials in the Roman Empire. The ornament on the wings has been compared with similar ornament on the Norrie's Law mounts (Figure 87) and the edge of the Norrie's Law pins. The ornament on the foot has also been seen by Dr Anna Ritchie to resemble a double-disc proto-symbol. (Drawings: L. Laing)

The suggestion that the symbol might have been a later addition to the pin, as some have argued, seems invalid, since the symbol appears to have been engraved on the back of the pin-head before the pin shank was fastened to it. Similar manufacturing hammer-marks appear on a number of the pieces in the Norrie's Law hoard, and it seems unlikely that all the objects were gathered up for scrap several hundred years after the date of their manufacture and use. If it is accepted, as most people are agreed, that the roundel with raised spiral bosses from the hoard could date back to the second or third century AD, a seventh-century deposition of the hoard would be very difficult to support, especially since it is extremely unlikely that Roman silver reached Pictland after the time of the Pictish raids on Britannia in the fourth century.

It has already been noted that the two silver plaques from the hoard bear Pictish symbols: a double-disc and Z-rod; and the forepart of a 'dog' (probably a seal). The plaques are quite plain on the back and were clearly never intended for attachment to anything. They are most readily explained as Pictish versions of the votive plaques (often leaf-shaped and sometimes silver) dedicated in Roman shrines.

The silver penannular ornaments were probably torcs. Originally worn round the neck by the pre-Christian Celts, the Norrie's Law examples would have been difficult to flex to admit the neck and were probably, therefore, worn as Roman officers wore them, as chest decorations.

The two hoards of silverwork are not the only silver finds with Pictish symbols on them. A series of twelve chains has come to light, mostly in southern Scotland outside Pictland, which in two cases have terminal rings with Pictish symbols on them. One of these was found in 1864 at Parkhill, Aberdeenshire. The symbols on it are however not 'orthodox' – at one extremity of the penannular terminal there are two red enamelled triangles with three enamelled dots between them, while at the other end there is an elongated s-shape flanked by two groups of three dots, also enamelled. An s-shaped figure does appear on some stones, but it does not take this form.

A second silver chain, found at Whitecleugh, Lanarkshire, has a similar 'napkin ring' terminal. This bears a double-disc and Z-rod at one end and a 'notched rectangle' at the other. The notched rectangle is of very unusual form, though it has its counterpart on a stone from Falkland, Fife, and the double-disc and Z-rod is similar to the symbol that appears on the plaques from Norrie's Law. Dr Isabel Henderson has suggested that, despite its discovery in southern Scotland, the Whitecleugh chain was decorated in Fife. She has also pointed out that there are similarities with the symbols on the cave walls at East Wemyss. There can be little doubt that the chains were 'symbols of power', and there is evidence from early medieval Welsh sources that chains were worn by kings there before crowns came into fashion. Dr Henderson has suggested that the concentration of finds in Lowland Scotland is to be explained by looting by the Anglo-Saxons of Northumbria in the second half of the seventh century, when they

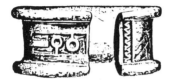

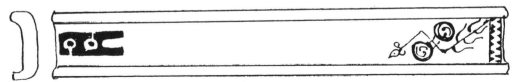

Figure 89 Terminal ring of silver chain, Whitecleugh, Lanarkshire. Massive silver chains appear to have been a symbol of rank among the Picts (the horseshoe-shaped symbols perhaps represent them). A few, such as this one, have terminal rings bearing symbols. The symbols are only readily matched in the East Wemyss caves in Fife, so perhaps this chain was looted from southern Pictland by Anglo-Saxons. (Drawing: L. Laing)

invaded and occupied southern Pictland. This seems very probable but, of course, does not provide a date for the chains which could have been much older.

One of the items in the Norrie's Law hoard is, as has been noted, a silver roundel with high-relief spiral bosses and a keeled crest. This may be older than the other objects in the hoard. Dr Henderson has suggested that the shoulder scrolls on Pictish symbol animals are derived from such embossed metalwork, and were intended not so much to indicate muscles as to represent volume. From this she has argued that the symbols were originally metal appliqués, either soldered to metal or sewn to cloth.

There might be some confirmation for the idea that the symbols were employed in metal foil in two finds. The first was a now-lost crescentic plaque from the Laws, Monifeith, Angus. This has a similar decoration to those which appear on the Norrie's Law plaques – a double disc and Z-rod symbol in conjunction with a dog or seal head. Like the Norrie's Law plaques, it could have been a Pictish version of a Roman votive plate. The back has a complex fret pattern, and an inscription in Viking runes inscribed by a later owner. Versions of double-disc symbols were also found in a Viking grave at Ballinaby, Jura. These have concentric circles of bosses on the round terminals, and pellets and triangles in the joining bars. They are made of tinned bronze and are in very bad condition, so it is not now possible to see how they were used, but they could have been sewn on to garments.

The Animal Art of the Pictish Stones

The animals that appear on the Pictish symbol stones are very distinctive, and display hip and shoulder spirals, ear-curls, truncated noses and great economy of line. They are at variance with most of the creatures

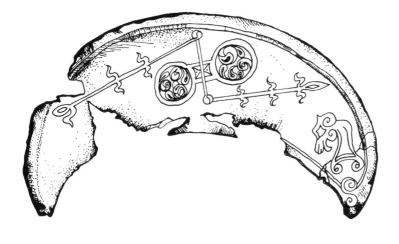

Figure 90 Both sides of a now-lost bronze plaque found at Monifeith, Angus, in the eighteenth century. It could have been a votive plaque for a shrine or an insignia. The symbols are the same as those on the Norrie's Law plaques. The inscription in runes was added by a Viking owner, apparently called Grimkitil. (Drawings: Angeline Morrison)

Figure 91 Double-disc terminals. Two pairs of double-discs were found in a Viking grave at Ballinaby, Jura. Made from thin tinned bronze, they are now very corroded – these are the two best preserved terminals which come from different pairs. They may have been votive plaques similar to the Monifeith example (see Figure 90), or may have been insignia worn on clothing, which is more likely. (Drawing: L. Laing)

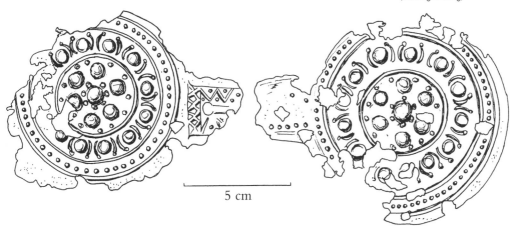

5 cm

that adorn Anglo-Saxon or Irish metalwork of the Dark Ages and, apart from the similarly naturalistic creatures in Insular manuscripts, as has been noted, they are not readily matched in early medieval art.

There are, however, a few fairly naturalistic creatures in early Anglo-Saxon art. Some appear on sixth-century Anglo-Saxon pots, for example on one from Spong Hill, Norfolk. In fifth-century Anglo-Saxon metalwork a few more occur, notably on metalwork current in Kent decorated in what is known as the 'Quoit brooch style'. A pair of confronted S-dragons, not unlike Pictish beasts, appear on an object from Croydon, while two further sea horses, similarly arranged on either side of a cross, decorate the mount for a hanging bowl from Faversham, Kent. Much closer to the Pictish symbols are the stag, bird and fish symbols that figure as appliqués on a hanging bowl from Lullingstone, Kent. Closer still are some creatures to be found in Romano-British art, for example the peacock, raven and fish that decorate the terminals of a penannular brooch from Bath, of the later fourth or fifth century. A late Roman brooch from Lydney, Gloucestershire, has a backward-looking crouched animal similar in style to some in Quoit brooch metalwork, both of which show strong affinities to a tradition of naturalistic animals found among the nomads of the Eurasiatic steppe. Professor Charles Thomas, who pointed to the similarities between some Pictish beasts and the art of the northern nomads, thought that this art was transmitted to Pictland in the pre-Roman Iron Age. Given, however, that nomad art was a major component of the art of Dark Age Europe, no doubt transmitted at the time of the migrations which were set in motion from just this direction, a fourth–fifth century context for nomad artistic influence is just as likely as an earlier one. Typical of nomad beasts are the hip and shoulder spirals, though these, as has been noted, are encountered in European art at many periods from the fifth century BC to the tenth century AD, if not later.

A naturalistic stag, in a style close to that of the Pictish symbols, has recently been noted on a rock-face at Eggeness, Galloway. Animals not unlike those on Pictish stones appear on Romano-British carvings.

Engravings of naturalistic animals also appear in a few other contexts in the early medieval period in the Celtic world: a stag can be seen at Dunadd on a motif-piece of the seventh or eighth century; there are figural designs from the Isle of Man and on motif-pieces from Tintagel, Cornwall (one of which depicts a dog chasing a stag); and on the cave walls of the King's Cove Cave on Arran, the designs include interlacing snakes of a type found on the Hunterston brooch of c. AD 700 and a figure with long hair parted in the middle, which recalls the 'man' symbol in the Book of Durrow (c. AD 650), apparently in the early Christian attitude of prayer. Professor Thomas has also pointed to naturalistic animals in Scottish Iron Age art, notably on potsherds from Kilphedir, Lewis.

From Portsoy, Banff, has come a double-headed whetstone which belongs to a group of ritual whetstones or sceptres, mostly known from

Figure 92 Whetstone from Portsoy, Banff. This was probably ceremonial and resembles pagan whetstones such as that from Sutton Hoo, Suffolk, which accompanied the rich burial of an East Anglian king. The Portsoy stone, however, appears to bear a Christian cross, and a fish which is the symbol of Christ in early Christian iconography. The worried heads are stylistically close to the pin from Golspie (see Figure 45). Height: 14.4 cm. (Drawing: L. Laing, after Smith)

Anglo-Saxon England. The heads on the Portsoy stone have furrowed brows, and the stone has engraved salmon combined with 'horseshoes', and what looks like a 'tuning fork' symbol. The furrowed heads are similar to the head on the Pictish silver pin found in a garden at Golspie, Sutherland (see Figure 45). The finest comparable whetstone came from the Anglo-Saxon royal burial at Sutton Hoo, and was deposited around 625, but could have been much older. There are other examples from Hough-on-the-Hill, Lincolnshire, (which has a fifth–sixth century pagan Anglian cemetery), and from Collin, Dumfriesshire. One without heads is known from Ulceby, Yorkshire, and one with a head has come from Llandudno, Gwynedd. The Sutton Hoo and Hough stones seem to have been made from greywacke from southern Scotland. The Llandudno whetstone has an interlace knot on it which may be secondary but which cannot date from much earlier than the eighth century.

A notable feature of the animals on the Pictish stones is that they are creatures that figure prominently in pagan Celtic religion. The four most important cult animals in the Celtic world were the horse, dog, boar and bull. The horse and dog (each usually represented by a head) are infrequent Pictish symbols, but the bull is slightly more common, especially at Burghead, Moray, where so many bull carvings (without other symbols) have been found on stones that it may even be inferred that there was a pagan Pictish bull cult there.

The horse as a cult animal goes back to the Bronze Age in Europe, and was associated in the Iron Age with the horse-goddess Epona.

Dogs are the attendants of several Celtic deities, for example Epona, sometimes the hammer god Sucellos, and the Three Mothers of Romano-British cult practice. In late Roman Britain, dogs were associated with the healing cult centre of Nodens at Lydney, Gloucestershire.

The bull or ox head was used to decorated the escutcheons of buckets from the Iron Age through the Roman period. Although some may have been intended to represent cows, and thus be appropriate to milking pails, there is little doubt they also had a supernatural meaning. One of the rarer Pictish symbols is a facing bullhead, which can be matched in a host of contexts from Iron Age and Roman Britain.

Boars have an equally long currency through the Continental Iron Age and through Iron Age and Roman Britain. They were a popular subject for coin types, and were important symbols of food, hunting and battle.

The stag, too, is a symbol of considerable antiquity. It was an important motif in Scythian art, and seems to have been current in Celtic art from the seventh century BC onwards, for example the stag-horned god Cernunnos figures in later Iron Age Celtic art. In Irish tradition the stag and the boar enticed heroes to the realms of the gods. Divine bulls changed into stags. In general, the stag epitomized the forests of the Celtic world, and also had a prosperity and fertility cult value.

The snake had both healing and warring aspects. In Irish tradition the hero Conall Cernach confronted a guardian snake at the gate of an enemy fort. It seems to have been a protector against war and the terror of death. A ram-headed snake frequently appears in pagan Celtic art. Although a ram-headed snake is absent from Pictish symbol art, a bull-headed snake appears intertwined with another of more orthodox aspect on a stone from Golspie, Sutherland.

Geese were associated with war, on account of their aggressive nature.

Eagles may have had sky symbolism. They were particularly popular in the Roman period owing to their coincidental association with Jupiter. They figure prominently on Iron Age coins.

The fish appears only occasionally in Iron Age Celtic cult art.

The wolf also occurs in pagan Celtic art, for example on Celtic coins.

One symbolic animal was not to be found in the woods, rivers and fields of Pictland. This was the creature usually termed the 'swimming elephant' or 'Pictish beast'. It has a long beaked snout, a crest and a tail. Bizarre though the swimming elephant is, its ancestry is fairly easy to trace. The crested bird head first made its appearance on Roman 'dragonesque' brooches of the later first to early second century AD. It next figured on a couple of pieces of around the same date or slightly later from Ireland: the Petrie crown and Bann disc. From then on the crested bird head appeared on several objects which carried the story on into the early medieval period. At some point the crested bird head appears to be grafted on to the body of a quadruped, or perhaps a hippocamp (seahorse; a seahorse, derived one supposes from a Classical manuscript source, appears on some Class II stones). A similar creature, executed in filigree, appears on the Hunterston brooch at the end of the seventh century.

The Meaning of the Symbols

If it can be accepted that the symbols were evolved over a period of time, perhaps from the later Iron Age through to the sixth or seventh century, and were incised on stone from perhaps the fourth or fifth century onwards, the next question must concern meaning and function.

As has been noted, the Pictish symbols appear not just on stones but on a variety of objects. Their meaning cannot therefore be purely funerary. However, there is some reason to suppose that some at least of the Class I symbol stones were in effect tombstones in the Roman tradition. The strongest evidence comes from the discovery of a stone associated with a burial at the Dairy Park, Dunrobin, Sutherland. Excavation here in 1977 suggested that a symbol stone had been erected on top of a cairn containing a cist made out of slabs in which had been laid the body of a woman. The associated stone bore a mirror and comb symbol, along with a snake and Z-rod and a double-crescent symbol. The discovery of the burial confirmed the long-held

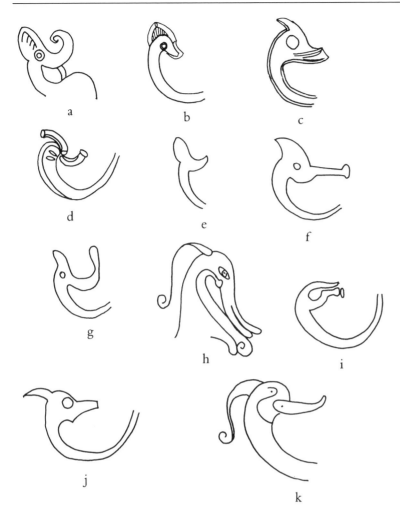

Figure 93 The 'swimming elephant' symbol and its relatives. (a) a Roman Brooch of the second century AD, Cirencester, (b) and (c) from the Irish Petrie Crown of a similar date, (d) from the Bann disc, Ireland, (e) from a bronze ball, Walston, Lanarkshire, (f) from a latchet, a type of dress-fastener, Ireland, probably sixth century, (g) from a hand-pin, Ireland, (h) Pictish symbol stone, (i) Sutton Hoo hanging bowl, (j) escutcheon of a hanging bowl, River Bann, Ireland, (k) Hunterston brooch. (Drawing: L. Laing)

instinctive belief that the mirror and comb symbol pair denoted a woman. Alongside this evidence can be set the discovery of symbol stones from five of a series of twelve rectangular and round cairns over-lying burials of laid-out skeletons. Although it is not possible to prove conclusively that the burials and stones are actually related, the likeliest explanation is that they were. Earlier finds also seem to point to the association between stones and burials. The Picardy stone from Insch seems to have been from the top of a cairn which in turn covered a burial, while a cist burial from Easterton of Roseisle had a symbol stone built into the cist.

Two points have been made about the location of symbol stones that are significant. First, the type of rectangular cairn with which some of the stones seem to have been associated may have an ancestry going back to a type of burial found in the pre-Roman Iron Age in

Yorkshire. Second, the distribution of the stones (beyond the Mounth at least, where this has been studied) seem to be close to water and on good agricultural ground, on a south-east- (or sometimes north-east-) facing slope. The cultic importance of water is a tradition that goes back to the pre-Roman Iron Age and probably even the later Bronze Age in Britain, and the sites chosen for symbol stones thus seem to have been locations long inhabited and venerated.

If some at least of the stones are tombstones, then it is reasonable to infer that regardless of when the symbols were invented, their carving on stone goes back to the point at which the Picts took up the idea of erecting tombstones, possibly from the Romans or the early Christians in the fifth century. A fifth-century cemetery with an inscribed tombstone lay just to the south of Pictland at Kirkliston, Edinburgh, for example. This was probably but one of many cemeteries with tombstones on the frontiers of Pictland in the fifth to sixth centuries.

The most logical interpretation of the symbols is that they are identifications of the dead, or personal inscriptions where they occur on portable objects or cave walls. They were, in effect, names and/or titles, giving cultural identity/ancestry or history.

Thus far most interpretations of the symbols are in agreement: there is less agreement on how they should be read.

F.C. Diack, in a study published after his death in 1944, argued that the symbols were indeed devised as tattoos and actually denoted the status of individuals. He drew attention to a text of Herodian, relating to the campaigns of Septimius Severus against the Caledonians in AD 208, in which Herodian said: 'They are ignorant of the use of clothes, and only cover their necks and bellies with iron which they think an ornament and sign of wealth as other barbarians do gold. They tattoo their bodies not only with likenesses of animals of all kinds, but with all sorts of drawings. And this is the reason why they do not wear clothes, to avoid hiding the drawings on their bodies.'

To this may be added a text from Isidore of Seville (AD 560–663) who, though writing relatively late, was contemporary with the continuing use of symbols and had access to older sources. In his Origines he wrote: 'The race of the Picts have a name derived from [the appearance of] their bodies. These are played upon by a needle working with small pricks and by the squeezed out sap of a native plant, so that they bear the resultant marks according to the personal rank of the individual, their painted limbs being tattooed to show their high birth.'

In the seventeenth century, Duald MacFirbis, drawing on a now lost source, wrote: 'The Cruithneach [Pict] is one who takes the cruths or forms of beasts, birds and fishes on his face; and not on it only, but on his whole body.'

Diack, in considering Tacitus' Agricola, 29, concluded that the obscure reference to Caledonian warriors, 'each one carrying his honours', was a reference to the status displayed in the form of tattoos. Diack went on to point out that an early Irish Law Tract refers to twenty-six classes, and this multiplicity of social grades would explain, in Diack's view, the range of symbols which, in the latest analysis, amount to twenty-eight pair groups (see p. 125).

In 1963 Professor Charles Thomas attempted to extend Diack's scheme by providing explanations for individual symbols. The animal symbols he saw as the totemic creatures of tribal groups, and the abstract symbols as indicators of status. In order to find interpretations for some of the abstract symbols he had to take imaginative though not implausible leaps. The notched rectangle, for example, was a bird's-eye view of a chariot, while the triple-disc was a similar view of a cauldron. A further leap explained the 'cauldron' as a magical symbol perhaps appropriate to a magus or wizard. Thus a stone with, for example, eagle and triple-disc symbols could be interpreted as the tombstone of a magus of the eagle tribe.

This interpretation, though intelligent, has not found favour. The real problem with equating animal symbols with tribes is that there is no particular regional distribution of specific animal symbols – they are found all over Pictland. If they were clan badges they would be expected to be found in particular concentrations. If one is to follow this line of reasoning, animal symbols should probably be seen as 'secondary rank symbols', qualifying the rank designated in the abstract symbols. The reason why they should not be seen as 'primary rank symbols' lies in the fact that animal symbols rarely occur without abstract symbols except where there are pairs of animals or in the case of the Burghead bulls, the Dunadd boar and, possibly, the Inverurie horse, which may have been carved for another purpose, but abstract symbols do appear without animals. It has already been suggested that particular animals had particular connotations in pagan Celtic religion, thus a boar symbol might equate with a warrior, a goose symbol with a seer, and so on.

It is amusing to speculate along these lines but, of course, one cannot get very far: at best these are only ill-informed guesses.

A second line of enquiry has been put forward by Dr Ross Sampson. He suggested that the symbols are hieroglyphs and are in fact name components. He suggested that Irish and Welsh personal name frequencies appear to match the frequencies with which symbol combinations occur on Pictish stones. He has gone on to suggest that some of the more obscure symbols are adjectival and that the names meant such things as 'wise eagle' or 'shining salmon'.

There are several objections to this theory, attractive though it is. If it is argued that each symbol represents a component of a name, it has to be said that some Pictish personal names have only one component, such as *Drest*. If, on the other hand, each symbol represents a syllable, as in normal hieroglyphs, it would suggest all Pictish personal names are disyllabic and made up of a combination of a limited variety of syllables. This again seems impossible, given names such as Talorcan. Further, one would expect common names to appear frequently, yet repeated combinations of the same symbols are not that common.

Figure 94 The slab from Golspie, Sutherland, combined incised figural work on one side and a relief cross on the other. Apart from Pictish symbols, the incised ornament includes a ferocious giant with an axe and knife, and a centaur-like creature. The axe is of a type fashionable in the Viking period and the stone probably dates from the eighth or ninth century. There is an ogham inscription along the edge. (Photos: RCAHMS)

There is also nothing to suggest that animal names are part of Pictish proper names. Dr Sampson has not yet, however, published his full analysis, and he may well have found solutions to these problems.

A final approach to the interpretation of the symbols is that taken by Dr Anthony Jackson, an anthropologist. Dr Jackson believes that the key to understanding the symbols lies in the idea that the Picts had an at least partly matrilineal society (see p. 58), a view that is not universally accepted. He is of the view that Pictish symbols are usually in pairs, and that where a single symbol occurs on a stone it is not a symbol (for example the Burghead bulls), the stone is broken, or it is a different sort of symbol. By studying the pairs he has estimated that there are twenty-eight. He has argued that the only time there are more than two symbols together are when they are combined with a mirror-and-comb, which he sees as a 'special' symbol providing information about the pair of symbols above it (i.e. explaining that they relate to a woman). On the basis of modern anthropological parallels he has suggested that the stones record marriage alliances between dynasties. His scheme does not apply to the Class III stones, but by that time, he suggests, the Picts had abandoned matriliny for patriliny and there was a break with the older rules of inheritance.

Dr Jackson's interpretation depends on two factors. First, it requires that the Picts possessed a matrilinear society but subsequently changed to a patrilineal one. That this major social upheaval coincides with the abandonment of Class II stones for Class III seems a little difficult to believe, as does any change as radical as this taking place within Pictish society without attracting notice. Bede was of the view that the Picts were partly matrilineal, therefore the changeover must have been after Bede's time. Second, the interpretation does not accept that any of the stones are tombstones, which is probably not the case, though of course it is not impossible that dynastic marriages (i.e. alliances) were recorded on tombstones.

Some of the problems may be reduced if it is allowed, as is probable, that the Picts were partly patrilineal, and that the symbols relate to both the male and female side of the marriage, as Dr Jackson has suggested. It has to be remembered that the stones probably commemorate only high-born Picts, and thus only a few ruling families are likely to be represented.

One final interpretation, advanced by Dr Isabel Henderson, is that the stones were territorial markers. This would seem to be disproved by the fact that some were tombstones and that the symbols cannot be related to territories.

Transitional Monuments

Lying stylistically between the Class I and Class II stones, there is a small group of monuments that combine incised symbols with other incised subject matter, or which have incised or very low-relief subjects without symbols.

There are two slabs in northern Scotland with incised figures carved using closely related techniques, one with accompanying Pictish symbols, the other without. The first is from Golspie, Sutherland. It has no less than seven symbols (and a possible eighth, if the intertwined snakes on the bottom are symbols), along with a bearded figure holding a knife and an axe. Along the edge is an ogham inscription which has been read as 'Allcallorred son of MacNu' and 'Uvan son of E . . . nn'. The second stone is the recently discovered slab from Barflat, Rhynie,

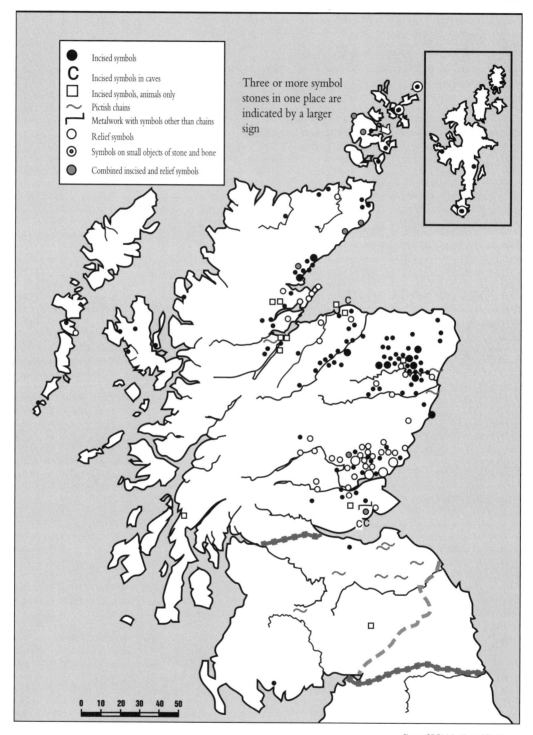

Incised symbols

C Incised symbols in caves

☐ Incised symbols, animals only

〰 Pictish chains

⌐ Metalwork with symbols other than chains

○ Relief symbols

◉ Symbols on small objects of stone and bone

● Combined inscised and relief symbols

Three or more symbol stones in one place are indicated by a larger sign

0 10 20 30 40 50

Figure 95 Distribution of Pictish symbols. Scale is in miles. (After Stevenson, with additions)

which has a similar figure holding a hammer. It has been suggested that this might be the Celtic smith-god Sucellos. On the Rhynie stone the haft of the hammer is represented by a single line, and a similar technique is used to indicate the shaft of knob-butted spears carried by figures (one of whom seems also to carry a square shield) on two other stones from Rhynie. Both are now extremely weathered. Despite its apparently 'early' style, the Golspie stone is richly decorated with relief on the back. Both stones probably date from the eighth century.

Perhaps one of the earliest of the stones with definitely Christian subject matter is one from Raasay, Skye, which is an outlier of the main series of stones. It has a crescent-and-V-rod and a tuning fork symbol, above which is a cross on a stem. Careful examination shows this not to be just a cross – it is a representation of a processional fan (or *flabellum*), and a hook on the top arm shows that it in fact is a Chi-Rho, the sacred monogram of Christ. A similar *flabellum* appears on the St Peter stone from Whithorn in Galloway, probably of the late seventh century, and on a stone from Inishkea North, County Mayo, Ireland. A stone from Iona has the same kind of hooked Chi-Rho cross but without the fan. Dating is not easy, but there is reason to suppose that the Chi-Rho of this type was introduced to Britain in the sixth century and remained current into the seventh. A recent study has shown that the same form of Chi-Rho was fashionable in Gaul from around AD 400 to the mid-sixth century, and that instances in Britain and Ireland belong to the sixth and seventh centuries, with perhaps a few extending into the early eighth.

Next to be considered is a fine stone from Papil, Shetland, which has a representation of a wheel-headed cross on a base decorated with a dog or, more probably, lion. On both sides of the cross-shaft are confronted pairs of clerics in 'duffel' coats, each holding a crozier, and one with a book-satchel round his neck. At the base are two bird-headed men with double axes and a head between their beaks. These latter have been interpreted, fairly plausibly, as a representation of the temptation of St Anthony by the birds. The lion is extremely close to the style of the lion evangelist symbol in the Book of Durrow, and the slab also has interlace, suggesting that a date around the middle of the seventh century is not impossible for it. The stone bears no Pictish symbols. A more sophisticated version of the cross-on-base subject can be seen on a later stone from Fowlis Wester, Perthshire. This combines incision with low relief.

The next stage in the development of Pictish sculpture seems to have involved the use of low relief, initially with incised symbols, then subsequently with symbols also in relief.

The first of these is the fine slab from Birsay, Orkney, which came from a Pictish cemetery site. It shows in relief three warriors with long robes, holding square shields and spears. Above, now badly damaged, are four incised symbols: a stemmed disc, a crescent-and-V-rod, a swimming elephant and an eagle. It was once thought that this stone

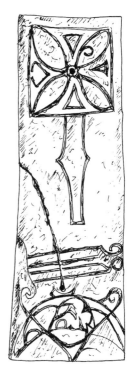

Figure 96 Raasay stone, Skye, probably seventh century. This bears a processional fan or *flabellum* with a Chi-Rho (monogram of Christ). It shows links with early Christian stones in Ireland. Height: 1.4 m. (Drawing: Amanda Straw, after Anderson, 1881)

was associated with a triple grave, but the evidence for this is not convincing. The presence of four symbols however makes it unusual. The treatment of the curly hair of the first of the procession of warriors is close to that in the Book of Kells, and a date approaching AD 800 is not impossible for this stone.

A few more 'transitional' monuments may be mentioned. A cross from Migvie, Aberdeenshire, has a very shallow-relief cross made from double-strand interlace, flanked by a double-disc and Z-rod, a horseshoe-and-V-rod, a pair of shears and a horseman, with a further horseman on the back. The style of the cross is not unlike some in Ireland, notably a slab from Clonmacnois, County Offaly, a stone at Gallen Priory, also County Offaly, and even closer a stone at Drumhallagh, County Donegal, which has double-strand interlace. In Ireland such slabs have usually been assigned to the seventh century, and the Donegal stones have been grouped with two very fine 'early' slabs at Fahan Mura and Carndonagh. Although various arguments have been advanced for dating the Carndonagh and Fahan Mura stones to the seventh century, this has recently been questioned and a date as late as the ninth century proposed for them. A ninth-century date might also fit the Migvie slab.

One of the finest shallow-relief stones is that at Glamis, Angus. Here the back bears three incised symbols – a snake, fish and mirror-and-comb – but the front has a relief cross with ogee armpits, flanked by an incised triple-disc and dog-head symbols, two figures in shallow relief fighting with axes, an axe-carrying centaur, a lion, and a suspended cauldron out of which human feet wave. The centaur is a refugee from some Mediterranean manuscript (or just possibly ivory) source, perhaps a World Chronicle. Careful study of the double-strand interlace on the cross-arms reveals that it is in fact zoomorphic. The cauldron evokes images of ritual drowning.

Of the other shallow-relief sculptures, particularly interesting is a Pictish rider drinking from a horn with a bird terminal, from Bullion, Invergowrie, Angus.

Before leaving the low-relief stones, mention should be made of another slab from Papil, Shetland, which may have been the front panel of a house-shaped shrine. It shows a free-standing cross on a base, three clerics in 'duffel coats' as on the other Papil stone (and like them holding croziers), another hooded figure on horseback and a final figure walking behind. A pattern of running scrolls makes up the ground. This has been interpreted as a version of the coming of Christianity to Shetland, but this seems highly unlikely. It possibly dates from the eighth century.

Figure 97 Papil stone, Burra, Shetland, possibly late seventh century. The shallow relief carving shows a lion, not unlike the evangelist figure in the Book of Durrow, and two bird-headed men with a human head between their beaks, perhaps a rendering of the temptation of St Anthony. Width: 53 cm. (Photo: Royal Museums of Scotland

Class II stones

The crosses that figure on a few of the preceding stones introduce the essential element of the design of the Class II stones. The 'transitional' stones may be assigned to the seventh and perhaps the earlier eighth

Figure 98 Migvie stone, Aberdeenshire. The symbols comprise a double-disc-and-Z-rod, an arch-and-V-rod and shears, with a faintly discernible mounted warrior. The back bears a mounted warrior. Despite the shallow relief and the fact that the interlace is similar to some on Irish stones attributed to the seventh century, the stone could be as late as the ninth century, since the symbols are in a late style and the shears are a very unusual symbol. Height: 1.4 m. (Photo: Tom Gray)

Figure 99 Glamis Manse Stone, Angus. The front (left) shows a richly interlaced cross, a seal head and triple-disc symbol. Above is a centaur with axes and a lion, while on the bottom left two axemen are engaged in a contest. Two figures are being dropped head first in a cauldron above. On the back (right) are incised a serpent, a fish and a mirror symbol. The cauldron scene may represent human sacrifice or execution. The triple-disc here lends support to the theory that it represents a cauldron seen from above. Height: 2.7 m. (Photos: RCAHMS)

century. The main series of Class II stones belongs to the eighth and ninth. The series begins with perhaps two of the finest, which carry on the tradition of low-relief carving. The best is the Aberlemno churchyard stone from Angus, one of a group of four or more stones (two others stand beside a road) from this centre. The front of the Aberlemno stone is a masterpiece of early eighth-century design.

The Aberlemno churchyard slab has a richly-decorated cross in low relief on the front, flanked by a zoomorphic scroll pattern, similar to Northumbrian 'vine scroll', a pair of interlocked long-legged, long beaked birds, closely matched in the Lindisfarne Gospels, a pair of confronted sea-horses, and a couple of contorted animals squashed into the top. The back, framed by two monsters, has a notched-rectangle and

Figure 100 Frontal slab from Papil, Burra, Shetland, probably from a corner-block shrine. This shows a cross and a procession of clerics. Length: 0.9 m. (Drawing: Amanda Straw)

Figure 101 The Aberlemno churchyard cross, Angus. This is the finest of the shallow-relief cross-slabs. The front (left) has long-legged, long-beaked birds similar to some found in the Lindisfarne Gospels, as well as other fantastic creatures. The back (right), which is framed by confronted monsters, shows a battle scene believed to represent Nechtansmere. Height: 2.3 m. (Photos: L. Laing, RCAHMS)

Z-rod and triple-disc symbols in relief at the top, and a battle scene beneath. The style of the front is very close to that of the Lindisfarne Gospels, suggesting a date around AD 700. It has been suggested that the battle on the reverse is that of Nechtansmere, fought in AD 685 some 10 km south of Aberlemno, when the Picts defeated and drove out the Angles who had been occupying southern Pictland. It has been pointed out that the warriors on the left of the stone are Picts; those on the right are differently attired, and have helmets not unlike that found at Coppergate, York, as well as chain-mail, which was found with the Coppergate helmet. Conventional dating has tended to put the stone late in the eighth century, but it need not much post-date the battle.

Dr Isabel Henderson has pointed out that, around 710, Nechton sent messengers to Jarrow in Northumbria asking for builders to be sent to build a stone church for him, and this was duly done. As the earliest sculpture in Northumbria appears to have been employed in the decoration of buildings, and as the designs for these sculptures were based on Insular manuscript patterns, it is likely that the Jarrow builders operating in Pictland introduced Insular designs similar to those found on the Aberlemno stone. A fragment of a wall panel from Monkwearmouth, a sister monastery to Jarrow in Northumbria, has ornament very like a detail on the Aberlemno stone, while interlace found in sculptures in the two monasteries are best matched in Pictland. Dr Henderson has suggested that it was through contact with Northumbria at this time that the Picts took up the cross-slab shape, and because they were reluctant to put symbols on a free-standing cross, continued to use slabs after the free-standing cross became popular elsewhere.

A closely related, if slightly less accomplished cross-slab, can be seen at Rossie Priory (Perth and Kinross). The Rossie Priory stone has a cross on both faces. That on the front is in higher relief than the supporting figures, as is the case on the Aberlemno churchyard stone. The symbolism is complex and difficult to fathom. At the bottom, on the left, two antlered beasts swallow the heads of two birds which in turn grasp the monsters with their claws. Above, a human (Jonah ?) is being eaten by a monster and a fish-tailed serpent. At the top there is a centaur and a bird-headed human attacking an animal with an axe. Beneath the cross-arm on the right, another dragon eats a snake coiled round (and through) its body, an ox stares out balefully beneath, while at the bottom are interlocked centaurs with snake's tails. It has been suggested that these creatures are derived from the monster-lore popular in Europe in the eighth and ninth centuries, and it has been mooted that the models may have been found in a book called the Marvels of the East, a copy of which was given to the Northumbrian king, Aldfrith by Abbot Ceolfrith, who had contact with the Picts. Similar monsters appear at

Figure 102 Rossie Priory stone, Perth and Kinross. The front (left), apart from a richly interlaced cross, displays a variety of strange animals including two intertwined centaurs and a sphinx, as well as a bird-headed man bearing an axe. On the back (right) the cross extends into the frame and there is a hunting scene, as well as two Pictish symbols above a push-me-pull-you animal. At the top the figure carrying birds may be a triumphant hunter, but is more probably a Pistish version of the Germanic story of Egil and the birds which appears on the Franks casket (see Figure 130). Height: 1.7m. (Photos: RCAHMS)

Dunfallandy, Gask, Woodwray, Inchbrayock, and on several stones in the collections at St Vigeans and Meigle. The stones are concentrated in southern Pictland, and may have been produced by a regional workshop tradition.

One other stone, from Eassie, Angus, has a cross in shallower relief than the two previously discussed but in the same general style, here flanked at the top by seraphim. On either side of the shaft is a warrior (David ?) with a spear and a square shield, and a stag hunt, to which the spear-carrying warrior may relate. On the back are a swimming elephant and double disc and Z-rod, a procession of three cloaked figures, a figure standing in front of a tree set in a base with human heads suspended from its branches, and some striding cattle.

A bridge between the earlier low-relief cross-slabs and the later, higher relief and more intricate stones is provided by a slab at Dunfallandy, Perthshire. The cross on the front has a square rather than a round central ornament, but is in higher relief than the supporting figures which include more fantastic beasts, perhaps from the Marvels of the East, and an angel (or rather a seraph) similar to those atop the Eassie stone. Bosses, probably

Figure 103 Eassie Priory stone. The front (left), which has a cross surmounted by angels, shows a long-legged hunter. The back (right) has a tree with human heads on it (a pagan shrine?), cloaked figures and symbols. (Photos: RCAHMS)

Figure 104 Dunfallandy stone, Perthshire. This extremely ornate stone belongs to the 'Boss' group of monuments, with bosses imitating metalwork. On the front (left) is a variety of animals including what may be a camel, perhaps derived from some manuscript source, as well as two angels. On the back (right), two monsters hold a human head between them and form a frame for the two seated figures with symbols above. Beneath, a rider accompanied by symbols rides over a group of hammer, anvil and tongs. Was this a monument to a smith? Height: 1.5 m. (Photos: Tom Gray)

derived from metalwork, however, decorate the cross, and are thus a foretaste of the 'Boss Style' monuments. The whole design is set in an interlaced frame. On the back a pair of monsters frame the design (as they did on the back of the Aberlemno churchyard cross), but here there are no less than eight Pictish symbols, a small Christian cross, the seated hermit saints – Paul and Anthony – and a cloaked rider.

The Boss Style Sculptures

After the low-relief crosses, the next group of monuments displays much higher relief and a far greater degree of elaboration. It is well represented among the collections of stones from St Vigeans, Angus, and Meigle, Perthshire. From this point in the development of Pictish symbol stones can be recognized on a typical Pictish cross-slab the front, dominated by a relief cross with armpits, infilled with complex interlace and other patterns, and flanked usually with figural work. The back is decorated with a variety of figures and animals combined with Pictish symbols. Although some seem to be of a narrative character, with a marked preference for hunting scenes, the arrangement of the figures appears fairly random for the most part, with no attempt at background, scale or perspective, though sometimes the ancient method of cavalier or stacked perspective may have been governing the design. The figures are mostly, but not invariably, from scriptural sources. In their choice of these the Picts seem to have avoided New Testament subject matter. Four themes predominate: episodes concerning David, representations of Jonah, and the stories of Daniel and

Samson. In addition, the hermit saints, Paul and Anthony, seem to have been popular. An undercurrent in the choice of Old Testament subject matter seems to have been the theme of salvation (hence Jonah and Daniel), and this preference was shown in other early Christian communities apart from the Picts. Manuscript models probably lie behind much of the basic iconography, though ivories and metalwork may also have contributed.

Much has been made of the influence of Northumbria on Pictish art but, as Isabel Henderson has noted, this has probably been over-emphasized, and she has pointed, in particular, to similarities in some cases to Mercian sculpture and manuscripts. As she has said, the richness of their iconography suggests that the Picts were in the mainstream of European artistic developments. The models seem to have been diverse, but the interpretation, in the final instance, is essentially Pictish.

A considerable diversity of forms is found in the shapes of the crosses – thirteen types have been recognized, of which those with round or double-square armpits are generally the most frequently encountered, and can be compared with 'carpet pages' in Insular manuscripts – indeed, the cross-slabs can be regarded as the sculptural counterparts of manuscript pages. To the more usual range the Picts added a type with quadrilobate nimbus, first seen perhaps on the stone from Aberlemno churchyard.

An even greater diversity of interlace patterns is apparent, some familiar from areas outside Pictland, others seemingly distinctively Pictish. There are indications that particular patterns had local distributions, and this implies regional centres of carving with their own pattern books.

Of the late eighth or early ninth century is the slab known as St Vigeans No. 7 from Angus. This slab has been cut down from its original size, but the front still has most of a fine interlace-decorated cross, with a series of running scrolls on the shaft decorated with triskele or 'Durrow' spirals of what close examination shows to be heads. At the top left and bottom right the heads are bearded and human, and alternate with slit-eyed snakes. In the centre, the four roundels have alternating spirals of bird and dolphin heads. The cross is flanked by the Hermit saints, Paul and Anthony, and two strange scenes of apparently pagan significance – on the left a man appears to be in the process of being dropped head first into a cauldron, while on the right a crouching figure holding a knife seems to be about to sacrifice a bull.

Of similar or slightly earlier date is the slab from Fowlis Wester, Perthshire. This too has what may be Saints Paul and Anthony, as well as a depiction at the top of Jonah and the Whale, and a finely interlace-decorated cross on a square base, generally similar to that on Meigle No. 7. The saints (or clerics) wear embroidered vestments and sit on what seem to be wicker chairs. A single-edged sword and a shield appear at the top.

Figure 105 St Vigeans No. 7, Angus. The most ornate of the St Vigeans collection of stones, the ornament on this monument (now damaged) includes whorls of alternating human and animal heads. The figural decoration appears to include a man being dropped into a cauldron, and two seated, confronted figures like those at Dunfallandy, here possibly identifiable as the hermit saints Paul and Anthony. Height: 1.7 m. (Photo: Scottish Development Department)

The ninth-century Class II stones may perhaps be seen to commence with the magnificent monument from Hilton of Cadboll, Easter Ross. It stands nearly 2.5 m high and is covered with a wealth of detailed ornament. Unfortunately the cross side is almost totally effaced by re-use, but the well-preserved reverse has three huge symbols at the top, a hunting scene with a female rider and accompanying trumpeters, and a pattern of trumpet spirals and inhabited vine scroll in the borders, which perhaps betray a connection with Mercian art of around AD 800. Such ornament is represented at Breedon in Leicestershire. The woman is designated by a mirror-and-comb symbol to her left. She rides side-saddle, and wears a penannular brooch. Her consort can be seen in profile behind her.

Of generally similar date is the third of the Aberlemno stones. This now stands beside the Class I symbol stone and is known as the Aberlemno roadside cross. It is about 3 m tall. The cross adorning the front is similarly tall and slender, with bosses in the armpits and with a pair of mourning angels with books on either side, as well as animal ornament. On the back the double-disc and Z-rod is paired with the crescent-and-V-rod in a similar style to the same pair of symbols on the Hilton of Cadboll stone. Beneath is again a hunt scene with attendant trumpeters, probably derived from David iconography, and at the bottom an episode from the story of David. Once again the closest parallel for the design is Mercian, and it is notable that both stones should have the same pair of symbols, though the Hilton of Cadboll stone seems to concern a female person, the Aberlemno stone a male. Despite their distance apart, both seem dependent on a similar pattern book.

Both these stones, and those described below, use round bosses decorated with interlace as part of their design. The ultimate inspiration for the bosses was probably metalwork, and the Boss Style monuments should be seen as inspired by free-standing high crosses, notably the eighth-century examples on Iona (see p. 148ff).

Several other boss-style monuments are outstanding. The first is the St Andrew sarcophagus, which was perhaps made to contain a relic of St Andrew brought to Scotland, so tradition has it, by St Rule in the time of Oengus. Whether Oengus is the eighth-century king of that name or, more probably, the ninth is unknown. In any event, the shrine, whatever its saintly connections, probably dates from the early years of the ninth century. It perhaps had a hipped roof (the modern reconstruction of it has one), as did smaller metal shrines, imitating a church or chapel. The panels were slotted into squared end-blocks, and as such it is the most sophisticated of a series of corner-post and corner-block shrines found in Britain and Ireland. The end panels have cruciform designs reminiscent of cross slabs, and the front has a figure of David fighting the lion with other episodes from the story of David in smaller scale: David on horseback is attacked by the lion, and beneath is David as warrior. A griffin at the bottom seems to be killing a mule,

Figure 106 Aberlemno roadside cross, Angus. This tall monument has Mercian-like angels flanking the central cross. The reverse has a hunting scene. It stands beside a Pictish Class I stone. Height: 2.8 m. (Photo: L. Laing)

Figure 107 Motifs from the slab from Birsay, Orkney. This is probably transitional between Class I and Class II stones. (Drawings: L. Laing)

and there are elements of a Pictish hunt scene in the accompanying animals. Surprisingly, for Pictish art, there is some foliage 'landscape'. The corner blocks carry intertwined animals. One of the end slabs has 'snake bosses' reminiscent of those on Iona crosses, as well as Eastern-looking monkeys. This is an outstanding work of European medieval art, and was found buried deep in the churchyard in 1833 near St Rule's (St Regulus') Tower. A strong connection can be seen in the figural work here and the figures in the Book of Kells, though Mercian

Figure 108 The St Andrews shrine. Regarded by many as one of the finest examples of Dark Age sculpture north of the Alps, this shrine belongs to a family of 'corner-block shrines' and may or may not have had a hipped roof making it resemble a metal shrine or chapel. The iconography relates to stories of David, and the style is close to that of the Nigg stone (see Figure 109). It dates from the early ninth century and may have been intended for a relic of St Andrew. Length: 1.75 m. (Photo: RCAHMS)

Figure 109 The Nigg cross slab, Ross. An outstanding example of 'Boss Style' art of around AD 800, this is closely related to the St Andrews shrine and in some of its details to the Book of Kells. The intricate ornament on the front (left) includes snake bosses, fret and animal lacertines. At the top, a dove holds a church wafer in its beak, between two figures (Saints Paul and Anthony) and two dogs. The badly damaged back (right) has David iconography. Height: 2.4 m. (Photos: RCAHMS)

influence is again apparent, especially in the vine scroll and the treatment of the draperies.

The Nigg cross, Ross, is a third early ninth-century example of the Boss Style. Now restored in Nigg Church, it stands 2.5 m tall. Snake bosses dominate the abstract ornament, and at its apex can be seen complex figural decoration relating to stories concerning Saints Paul and Anthony. Damaged David imagery decorates the back. The style of the figures with deeply channelled draperies is close to that of the St Andrews shrine, and the intertwining creatures on the arms of the cross are not unlike those on the Mercian ivory Brunswick casket. The key pattern on the stem of the cross (which also appears at Hilton of Cadboll) is a Mercian decorative feature, as is the all-over trumpet spiral decoration that occurs in a panel on the Hilton of Cadboll stone, and which can be matched on a slab from South Kyme, Lincolnshire.

After this group of Mercian and Kells-influenced monuments, the later Boss Style creations are to be seen at their best in the collections of stones at Meigle and St Vigeans.

Meigle No. 2 is an imposing stone standing 2.5 m high. It is somewhat weathered, but this fact has not destroyed its monumentality and wealth of decoration. The sides have lateral 'pegs', and it is not impossible that this was once the central panel of a stone triptych or screen, copying some wooden or, more probably, metal model (the multiplicity of bosses on the head suggests a metalwork design). Technically, this stone belongs to Class III, since there are no Pictish symbols on it, but otherwise the design is in the mainstream of Pictish art. On the back a hunting scene occupies the top; beneath it is Daniel in the lion's den, and beneath that a centaur holding a double-axe dragging a branch. At the bottom a figure watches a contest between animals. High-relief animals are also to be found on the front. The ancestry of the design lies with the Hilton of Cadboll and Aberlemno roadside slabs.

In northern Pictland, over-elaborate monuments were erected in a later ninth-century last fling of the Boss Style; in the South the latest Boss Style monuments were more restrained. St Vigeans No. 1 abandons bosses completely. It has an interlace-filled cross with a seraph standing on one arm (its opposite number is missing) and an assortment of flanking animals. On the back are Pictish symbols with a variety of animals, including a fearsome bear, a horned monster, a bird carrying a fish (probably symbolic of Christ carrying the soul) and a caped hunter attacking a boar with a crossbow. Of exceptional interest is the panel at the bottom of one side, beneath interlace decoration. It carries an inscription commemorating Drosten, Uoret and Forcus. Accordingly, the stone is also known as the Drosten stone. Drosten is a Pictish form of the name Tristan, which in itself is Pictish in origin. Vine scroll of Anglo-Saxon derivation decorates the other side.

After the Triumph of Dalriada

Following the unification of the Picts and the Scots under Kenneth Mac Alpin around 843, sculptures continued to be produced in Pictland, but mostly without symbols. These Class III monuments are a varied collection, mostly undistinguished.

Two, now in Brechin Cathedral, Angus, should be mentioned. The first, from Aldbar, has a weathered pair of facing figures on a bench at the top, David and the Lion, a staff, a harp and some animals. The facing figures are a feature of very late sculptures in Pictland. For

Figure 110 Meigle No. 2, Perthshire. Despite its weathering, this huge cross-slab is an outstanding achievement of Pictish art. Perhaps the central element in a stone triptych (which would explain why the hunting scene on the back is incomplete), its iconography includes Daniel in the Lion's den, strange animals, and a centaur carrying an axe and a branch. Height: 2.5 m. (Photo: RCAHMS)

example, they appear on a stone from Elgin, which also has a pair of fighting creatures which can be compared to those on one of the 'pepperpots' in the St Ninian's Isle treasure. Less plausibly similar creatures adorn a slab from Colerne, in Wiltshire, a stone known as St Vigeans No. 11, and a slab from Invergowrie, Angus, which similarly has crossed St Ninian's Isle beasts with snub snouts.

The second Brechin stone is a rectangular slab (originally a more substantial block) in Northumbrian style (as arguably are the preceding monuments with facing figures), with a cross containing the Virgin and Child and a Hiberno-Saxon inscription: S MARIA MR XPI ('St Mary, Mother of Christ'). There are also supporting figures and a bird on the upper arm of the cross, possibly an unconvincing dove. Abstract ornament is absent.

A short, broken cross-slab from Kirriemuir, Angus, has more facing figures in the same style, a mirror-and-comb symbol and a seated figure on a chair with animal heads on the back. This may be the last stone to have been carved with symbols. Another, more substantial slab from Kirriemuir may be of slightly earlier date, with a tiny Pictish symbol on the back and more hunting and David iconography.

The last fling of Pictish sculptural art was a triumphal one in the form of Sueno's stone, which stands near Forres, Elgin. This 6.5 m

Figure 111 The Book of Deer, ninth century. This small book is related to the Irish 'pocket gospels', and was probably executed in Pictland by an artist who had seen a manuscript model but did not have it in front of him. It shows certain similarities to the style of a Pictish stone from Elgin. Dimensions: 15.4 x 10.7 cm. (Photo: Cambridge University Library)

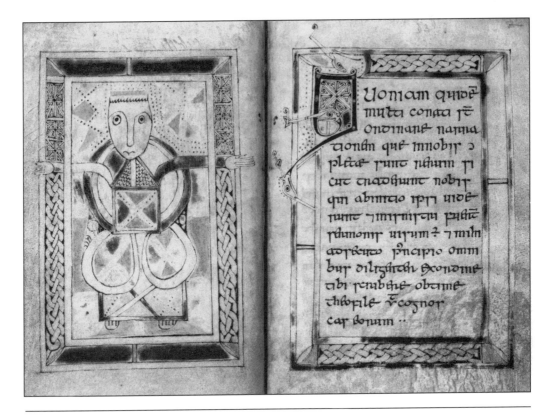

high shaft is the tallest in Scotland. Discovered in the eighteenth century after it had been buried, the name is an eighteenth century invention, as is the tradition that it was erected to commemorate a victory over the Vikings, though that is a possible explanation. The cross on one side is covered with tight interlace, as is its background. The back has a complex battle scene. Four unequal panels show cavalry, foot soldiers and executed prisoners. The figure panels recall tenth-century Irish high crosses (the patterning is reminiscent of the Muiredach cross, Monasterboice, for instance), and a date in the tenth century rather than the ninth is likely. Dr Anna Ritchie has suggested it may commemorate the killing of the Scottish king, Dubh, by the men of Forres in 966, to replace him with his cousin.

One manuscript survives from this period – the Book of Deer. This was probably produced in Pictland, perhaps at Deer, where it was revered by monks of the eleventh and twelfth centuries as their finest possession. It is in the tradition of 'pocket Gospels' produced in Ireland, and the treatment of figures on a Pictish stone from Elgin is so close to the similar treatment of figures in Deer that it is very likely the scribe was familiar with this or some other Pictish stones. It has been suggested that the book was produced by an experienced scribe who had seen an illuminated Gospel book but had only sketches from which to work.

Pictish Metalwork

Attention has already been drawn to the silverwork from the Norrie's Law hoard. There is quite a variety of ornamental metalwork from Pictland, including an array of silverwork, which must have been produced from metal looted from Roman Britain. Sometimes Romano-British models provided the inspiration for Pictish products. Hanging bowls, for example, which were first produced in Roman Britain and continued thereafter to be made in the Dark Ages, were as popular with the Picts as with their more southerly neighbours.

Part of a hanging bowl with openwork escutcheons for taking the suspension rings was found at Tummel Bridge, Perth, associated with a series of large, virtually plain penannular brooches in beaten silver that seem to have been inspired by Irish models.

Another fragmentary hanging bowl comes from Castle Tioram, Moidart, while the mould for making a similar escutcheon came from excavations in the Pictish fort at Craig Phadrig, Inverness.

Of somewhat later date, a broken escutcheon (actually the mount which was affixed to the bottom of the bowl) with rich enamel decoration was found at Aberdour, Fife. The central decoration of a cross, with wavy nimbus, shows it belongs to the period after the conversion of the Picts, but the ornament includes a panel of angular interlace and a Pictish-looking animal.

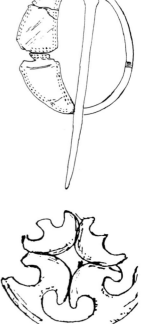

Figure 112 Items from a hoard, Tummel Bridge, Perthshire, probably seventh century. This cache comprised fragments of a hanging bowl with openwork escutcheons of a type known to have been made in Scotland, a fragment of a bronze cup and a series of beaten silver penannular brooches decorated with a two-pronged implement. Brooch diameter: 7.5 cm. (Drawing: L. Laing)

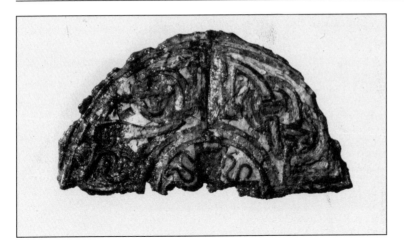

Figure 113 Enamelled bronze escutcheon of which only half survives. This was probably the basal disc for a hanging bowl. The ornament includes interlace, a central cross and a Pictish-like animal. It was found during clearance at Aberdour Castle, Fife. Diameter: 4.3 cm. (Photo: Royal Museums of Scotland)

A small enamelled mount, perhaps from a casket, was among the finds from the Pictish fort at Clatchard Craig. The decoration is distinctly Roman-looking with a pattern of peltas not unlike those on hanging bowls. The same site has produced a series of clay moulds for casting penannular brooches and pins, including the mould for a penannular with flaring terminals and ornament not unlike that found on a surviving silver brooch from Cluny Castle, Perthshire.

Several sites have produced clay moulds for metalwork, the largest collections coming from Clatchard Craig, Fife, and Birsay, Orkney. By far the largest number of moulds and surviving pieces of metalwork are items of personal adornment, particularly penannular brooches. Penannular brooches originated in pre-Roman and Roman Britain.

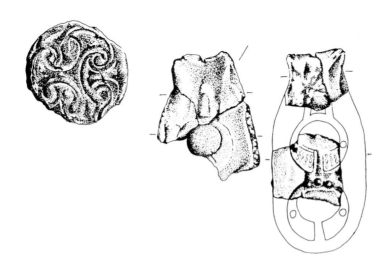

Figure 114 Bronze mount and moulds, Clatchard Craig, Fife. The mount was for a disc decorated with three back-to-back C-scrolls, originally with an enamelled ground. The mould was for casting penannular brooches. Disc diameter: 2.3 cm. Brooch diameter: 27 cm. (Drawings: Gwen Seller)

143

Figure 115 Terminal of a penannular brooch. This fine brooch was unfortunately broken on discovery in the nineteenth century at Dunbeath, Caithness, and only this terminal survives. The gold filigree animal is set in a tray on the silver ground. This technique is characteristic of a number of early pieces of richly ornamented jewellery, including the Hunterston brooch. It is likely to have been produced in either Dalriada or Pictland at the end of the seventh century. Width: 7.2 cm. (Photo: Royal Museums of Scotland)

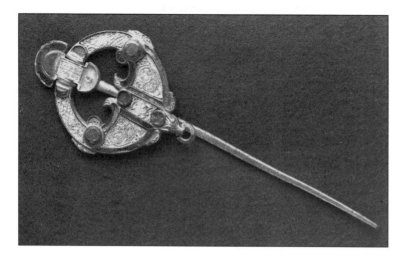

Figure 116 The Westness Brooch, Rousay, Orkney. This superb brooch is of a type known as a 'hinged pin', developed in Ireland in the ninth century. Of silver with gold and amber inlays, it could have been produced in Dalriada. Note the fine wolf-head at the bottom of the hoop. Length: 17.5 cm. (Photo: Royal Museums of Scotland)

Figure 117 Fragmentary bronze mount with Pictish-style wolf. This was found with the Westness brooch in a Viking woman's grave at Westness, Orkney. The snub-nose is Pictish. Dimensions: 6.6 x 3.2 cm. (Photo: © Trustees of the National Museums of Scotland)

They comprise, as the name suggests, a hoop with a break through which a pin can pass to grip the cloth, the pin being swivelled on the hoop. Although there is a great diversity of Pictish penannular brooches, they are all true penannulars and are characterized by having a characteristic type of panel on the loop, distinctive pins and, very frequently, lobed terminals. A typical form has a pair of confronted dragon heads for terminals. Made in both silver and bronze, the finest are perhaps a silver-gilt brooch recently found in a fort at Aldclune, Perthshire, which has round terminals, and the brooches from two hoards of later silverwork, from Rogart, Sutherland, and from St Ninian's Isle, Shetland.

The Rogart brooches seem to have come from a large hoard which included a pair of Anglo-Saxon ninth-century strap-ends and a couple of smaller brooches as well as two large ones. The finest is of silver gilt. It is decorated with three-dimensional bird heads rivetted on to the terminals and the pin, giving the impression that they are pecking from the brooch.

The finest works of Pictish metalwork, however, can be seen in the St Ninian's Isle treasure, discovered in 1958 under the chancel arch of a tiny medieval church on a tidal island off the coast of the Shetland mainland. The St Ninian's Isle treasure comprises a silver hanging bowl, a series of beaten silver bowls, twelve penannular brooches, three pepperpot-shaped objects, a sword pommel, two sword chapes, a spoon and a pronged implement, along with the only item not of silver – the jawbone of a porpoise. The whole seems to have been deposited around AD 800, perhaps in fear of a Viking raid. Several of the brooches are worn. Perhaps the most interesting is one with dragon-head terminals, their teeth bared menacingly. All the objects in the hoard are Pictish, with the possible exception of the hanging bowl which has been seen as Northumbrian and somewhat earlier than the other objects in the find. But as has already been noted, the Picts made hanging bowls, and there are features in the ornament which point to a Pictish origin for this too, though Anglo-Saxon influence is undeniable. The use of a hatched background to the animals on the roundel on the base of the bowl is matched on the pronged implement from the hoard, while on the underside the stamped triskele-decorated mount is in the mainstream of British, rather than Anglo-Saxon, bowls. The spoon has a delightful dog's head licking from the bowl. The seven bowls have punched dot decoration including cavorting, tail-biting animals. Of particular interest is the rich, chip-carved ornament on the 'pepperpots' (probably sliding strap-adjusters for a sword harness), which combine both Celtic abstract ornament and animal ornament with interlace backgrounds. Impressive, too, are the two sword chapes, ending in snub-nosed Pictish animal heads. One carries an inscription in Irish lettering, possibly naming a Pict: 'Resad son of Spusscio'. This has also been read as: 'property of the son of the Holy Spirit'. Some of the animal ornament shows close affinities to creatures found in Pictish sculpture.

Figure 118 The larger of the two main silver gilt brooches surviving from the Rogart hoard, Sutherland, found in 1868 (one of the eleven recorded is in Edinburgh, two others, damaged, are in Oxford). This brooch is an outstanding example of Pictish metalwork, with bird heads made separately and rivetted on. The design is typically Pictish. Diameter 12 cm. (Photo: Royal Museums of Scotland)

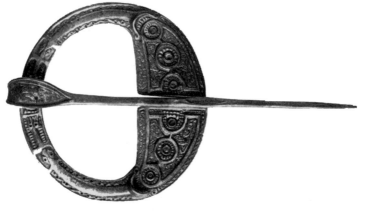

Figure 119 This fine silver brooch was found near Clunie Castle, Perthshire. It shares features with some Irish brooches of the Viking Age, but the layout of the terminals is matched on a mould from Clatchard Craig, Fife, and the pin is purely Pictish in style. It may be later ninth century. Diameter: 11.5 cm. (Photo: Royal Museums of Scotland)

Figure 120 This dragon-headed brooch from the St Ninian's Isle treasure is the only one in the find of its kind, though other dragon-headed brooches are known from Pictland, one from Freswick, Caithness, and a series from moulds found at Birsay, Orkney. Diameter: 7.1 cm. (Photo: Royal Museums of Scotland)

Figure 121 St Ninian's Isle treasure, 'pepperpots'. The St Ninian's Isle treasure was found in 1958 under the chancel arch of a small church on a tidal island. It comprises the most important collection of Celtic treasure from Britain. The so-called 'pepperpots' are probably belt adjustors for a sword harness. The largest is 4.3 cm high. All three are richly decorated. (Photo: © The Trustees of the National Museums of Scotland)

A curious feature of the hoard as a whole is the affinity some of the objects appear to have with Roman models. Could some Roman treasure hoard have survived to inspire the design?

Another, lost, hoard of silverwork from Burgar, Orkney, was probably of the same date. The objects from it included silver combs.

The Pictish type of brooch was popular outside Scotland. Pictish brooches (or fragments of them) have been found in York, Wales, Norway and Ireland, where they were influential in the design of Irish brooches.

Figure 122 Silver bowl, St Ninian's Isle, Shetland. One of a series of bowls from the find, this is decorated with a procession of Pictish-style animals. Like most of the objects in the hoard it dates from the late eighth century, and was probably buried in the face of a Viking raid around AD 800. Diameter: 14.4 cm. (Photo: © The Trustees of the National Museums of Scotland)

The engraved and punched decoration in the St Ninian's Isle treasure might suggest that three other objects originated in Pictland. The first is a censer found in a Viking grave in Bergen, the second a decorated pail from the Viking ship burial at Oseberg and the third the Monymusk reliquary.

The Monymusk reliquary is a tiny wooden box with a lid in the form of a hipped roof, covered with metal plates and with binding strips and mounts. It is one of a family of house-shaped shrines, best known from Ireland and from Viking graves to which they were taken as plunder from the Celtic realms, though similar house-shaped shrines were made in Anglo-Saxon England and on the Continent. The Monymusk Reliquary is also known as the 'Brecbennoch of St Columba', and was used as a battle standard. For example it was taken before the Scottish army at the Battle of Bannockburn when the English were soundly beaten in 1314. Monymusk has one surviving enamelled 'hinge' to take a carrying strap -- such reliquaries seem to have been carried round the neck – and a 'ridgepole' terminating in hooked-beak bird heads. The mounts on the lid and front of the box are arranged alternating round and square (some are now missing), and a similar design can be seen on another reliquary from Bologna, which may also have emanated from Scotland. A pair of similar hinges and a round mount of like design to the Bologna one are known from Viking burials in the western isles of Scotland.

It is only the engraved animal decoration with its background of punched dots that suggests the Monymusk Reliquary is Pictish, since the ornament is similar to that on the St Ninian's Isle bowls. It is not, however, impossible that the reliquary was made on Iona, on the occasion of the enshrinement of St Columba in the eighth century, which would fit the likely date of its style.

Sculpture in Dalriada

While these developments were taking place in Pictland, a separate tradition of sculpture is discernible in Dalriada.

The earliest inscribed monuments in Dalriada are grave-slabs from Iona, but the true beginnings of Dalriadic sculpture can be seen in the earliest of the Iona high crosses, St John's cross, St Martin's cross and St Oran's cross.

The earliest free-standing crosses in Western art are Northumbrian, and comprise the Ruthwell and Bewcastle crosses. Ruthwell now lies in Dumfriesshire, but in the seventh century this area was part of Northumbria. Before these were erected, timber free-standing crosses may have been set up in Northumbria, and through Northumbrian influence may have been erected on Iona too – the Northumbrian king, Oswald, is recorded as having set up a wooden cross prior to the battle of Heavenfield in 635. Free-standing wooden crosses certainly

Figure 123 St John's cross, Iona, eighth century. Arguably one of the earliest of the high crosses from Britain or Ireland, this is now restored from fragments. Note the birds' nest bosses, derived from metalwork. (Photo: RCHAMS)

seem to have been set up on Iona by the time of Adomnan, as he mentioned them.

The work on the Iona crosses is experimental. In contrast to the stones in Pictland there is little or no figural work apparent on the earliest, and their ornament appears derived from the art of the metalworker, the bosses recalling studs, and the cabled borders the binding strips on reliquaries. Particularly distinctive of the Iona crosses are the 'bird nest' bosses, which may be modelled on a type of boss in granular work found on the Irish 'Tara' brooch and Ardagh chalice.

Perhaps the most accomplished is St John's cross. Originally designed without a ring, it has the double-curved profile to its arms that is found in the Ruthwell cross in Dumfriesshire, and may be modelled on such Northumbrian prototypes. The cross seems to have been damaged in an early fall, and was repaired and strengthened with a ring which was slotted into the head using carpentry techniques. Once introduced, the ring with its connotations of a halo gained favour, and appears on subsequent crosses in both Britain and Ireland. The multiplicity of bosses shows affinities with Pictish cross-slabs, but the main inspiration are the bosses found in metalwork, though their arrangement on the cross is

Figure 124 St Oran's cross, Iona. Although very fragmentary, this is probably the earliest of all the high crosses. (Photo: RCHAMS)

probably governed by theological considerations rather than by the metal prototypes.

St Oran's cross, similarly fragmentary, is made from local stone unsuited to monumental carving. This is in contrast to the other two which were carved from imported blocks, some would say later. Apart from the familiar snake bosses, St Oran's cross introduces figural work, including a Virgin and Child, not unlike that which appears in a full-page illustration in the Book of Kells. A man with a quadruped may represent Daniel. A pair of rampant beasts, back-to-back with their heads forwards to face one another, with two smaller animals beneath, adorn the front of the upper arm.

Figure 125 St Martin's cross, Iona. The third of the ealier free-standing crosses of Iona, this has sockets in the arms, probably for detachable wooden extensions. It has snake bosses and some figural ornament. (Photo: RCAHMS)

St Martin's cross is the most intricate and the best-preserved of the three. The ornament on the front is abstract (apart from serpents and some creatures at the top), but on the back is a wealth of figural decoration with again a Virgin and Child in the centre of the crossing, rampant beasts similar to those on St Oran's cross at the top, and David and the sacrifice of Abraham on the shaft. St Martin's cross has truncated arms, as originally there were wooden extensions which were slotted in (the slots can still be seen) and perhaps removed in high winds.

All three crosses show strong affinities with two similarly experimental crosses at Ahenny in County Tipperary, though on the Ahenny crosses all figural work is confined to the bases. Whether one puts the Ahenny or Iona crosses first in the sequence, all belong to the later eighth century.

Of the remaining crosses on Iona, mention should also be made of St Matthew's cross. Only the bottom of the shaft survives. This is decorated with a key pattern, and Adam and Eve with the serpent, in a

Figure 126 The Kildalton cross, Islay, is an outlier of a group of monuments and was probably executed by a sculptor from the monastery. It shares figural work, including a Virgin and Child, with St Martin's cross on Iona. (Photo: RCAHMS)

manner which recalls the treatment of the subject on some Irish crosses. The cross probably dates from the later ninth or early tenth century.

The Iona school of sculptors seems to have been responsible for another fine cross, that at Kildalton on Islay. The Kildalton cross is very close stylistically to St Martin's and shares figural work, including a Virgin and Child. The Virgin was not taken up by the Irish sculptors.

A cross at Keills, Argyll, though related to the earlier Iona crosses, is perhaps slightly later. A bird's nest boss dominates the centre, and there is high-relief figure carving. Like St Martin's cross, its arms appear curiously truncated, but this seems to be part of the original design.

Of the later Dalriadic sculptures, mention may be made of an outlier in Pictland, the Dupplin cross. This is a hybrid monument – the sculptors were clearly trained in a Pictish tradition, and the warrior with a long, droopy moustache that appears on the shaft of the cross has his counterpart on a Pictish slab from Benvie and on the arch from Forteviot, Perthshire. The Dupplin cross has double curved arms, and beneath the mounted warrior is a procession of shield-bearers. A vestigial hunt can be made out below. Acanthus foliage on the head betrays its late date and its connections with contemporary Anglo-Saxon and Frankish work.

If the Dupplin cross represents a Dalriadic type of monument in Pictland, the last Dalriadic sculpture to claim attention represents a Pictish type of monument in Dalriada. This is the slab from Ardchattan, Argyll, which comprises a strange pastiche of elements. Flanking the cross are three hooded musicians, with harp, pan-pipes and rattle. Above are two animals, and below a facing warrior with a spear and notched rectangular shield. A human figure on the top has a lower body which turns into interlace, and there is a flanking, contorted animal. The ornament on the cross itself combines Durrow-style interlace with an all-over scroll pattern which in Pictland has been equated with Mercian influence. It probably belongs to the early ninth century.

Manuscripts and Metalwork in Dalriada

Thus far we have examined sculptures that are unlikely to have been moved very far from the place in which they were carved. The same cannot be said for manuscripts and metalwork, which are easily transportable. In the seventh century and later, a series of fine manuscripts was produced in Britain and Ireland. This is generally designated 'Insular', since the manuscripts are different from contemporary examples produced on the Continent, except for a few made by emigrants from Britain and Ireland. While some of these Insular manuscripts can be assigned on internal evidence and by common consent to a particular place or region – such as the Lindisfarne Gospels, which is known to be a Northumbrian manuscript of the period around AD 700

Figure 127 Keills cross, Knapdale. An outlier of the Iona School of crosses, this eighth-century monument has high-relief modelling and figural work, as well as a central boss. (Photo: RCAHMS)

and made almost certainly at Lindisfarne, or the Book of Armagh, accepted as having been made at Armagh in Ireland around AD 807 – much less certainty is attached to arguably the two most important Insular manuscripts: the Book of Durrow and the Book of Kells. While no one has yet suggested that the Book of Kells was Northumbrian, not everyone is convinced that it was made in Ireland, and the earlier Book of Durrow has been assigned both to Northumbria and to Ireland in the past. There is strong evidence, however, to suppose that both great Insular books were made in northern Scotland, in the lands of the Picts and Scots.

Manuscripts from the Mediterranean probably reached early clerics in Britain and Ireland soon after the conversion. However, none has survived, apart from a page from a late Roman book said to have belonged to St Augustine which has been dated to the sixth century, and which is probably Italian. Irish monks in the sixth century, who had established monasteries in Italy at centres such as Bobbio, soon started copying and embellishing manuscripts in their own style. But the earliest Insular manuscript is a Gospel book traditionally supposed to have been written and ornamented by St Columba, known as the Cathach (the 'Battler'). Although there is no proof, in terms of date the Cathach could have been made by St Columba, and was likely to have been written in a scriptorium on Iona. The decoration is confined to some initials, but in one can be seen a creature not totally unlike a Pictish swimming elephant.

After the Cathach, the next stage in the development of manuscript art comes with a Northumbrian work now in Durham Cathedral, the Durham Ms A II 10. This manuscript uses an elaborate initial letter with the essential ingredients of Insular art – spirals, peltas and confronted trumpet patterns, as well as a panel of simple interlace. It dates from around the second quarter of the seventh century, and bridges the gap between the Cathach and the Book of Durrow.

The Book of Durrow is a tiny volume compared with later ones, measuring 24.5 x 14.5 cm. The decoration in the Book of Durrow is relatively simple. First there are full-page illuminations with the symbols of the evangelists: calf, lion, eagle and man. Next, facing these pages, are elaborate initials ornamenting the first page of each gospel. In addition there are full-page decorations known as 'carpet pages', with a central cross, and finally there is a page with all four evangelist symbols in the angles of a cross.

There are three possible places where the Book of Durrow could have been produced: Durrow in Ireland, Lindisfarne in Northumbria, or Iona. No clue is provided by the palaeography as to where it was written. To decide, it is necessary to turn to the decoration of the manuscript.

The first thing to note is that the evangelist symbols are very close in style to Pictish Class I symbol beasts. For some, this fact has prompted the suggestion that Class I animals were derived from such Irish or

Figure 128 Ornamental initials from the Cathach of St Columba, perhaps executed on Iona in the late sixth or early seventh century. (Drawing: L. Laing)

Northumbrian manuscript sources as this. But Dr Henderson has pointed out that the hip and shoulder spirals of the Pictish animals show an understanding of anatomy that the Durrow versions do not. In other words, the Durrow beasts are inspired by Pictish art, not the other way round. Also Pictish is the use of dotted infilling as background to some letters. This type of infilling is found in metalwork, in particular in the Monymusk Reliquary and the St Ninian's Isle silver bowls, discussed earlier (p. 147 ff). On the Pictish Papil stone, too, can not only be seen the first cousin of the Durrow lion, but also a cross of arcs, very similar to one in the centre of folio 85v in the Book of Durrow.

If some elements in the Book of Durrow are Pictish, then others are Anglo-Saxon. It has long been acknowledged that the long-jawed biting creatures on folio 192v are derived from Anglo-Saxon metalwork. The creatures in the Book of Durrow have ankle-bracelets, which are found in the East Anglian royal burial at Sutton Hoo, Suffolk (on a drinking horn mount), and on a few other seventh-century pieces. The calligraphic style of the Durrow animals is also Anglo-Saxon and is matched by the style of those on the back of a brooch from Faversham, Kent. Also Germanic is some of the Book of Durrow's interlace – single-strand with red dots (probably imitating filigree wire in metalwork). This is excessively rare in Ireland (only occurring on a silver paten from the Derrynaflan hoard), but is slightly more common in England.

The third element in the repertoire of ornament in the Book of Durrow is of Romano-British derivation. This can best be matched by the ornament on the decorative discs for a series of hanging bowls found in the sixth and seventh century, mostly in Anglo-Saxon graves, though there seen as British (or Celtic) rather than Anglo-Saxon products. If the Book of Durrow was produced in Ireland, why should it be so strongly influenced by Pictish and Anglo-Saxon art, which at this stage was having a minimal effect on Irish art?

If the Book of Durrow was not made in Ireland, could it have been made in Northumbria? First, prior to the beginning of the eighth century it is unlikely, for historical reasons, that Pictish art had much impact on Northumbria. Second, the man symbol in the Book of Durrow has a 'Celtic' tonsure. Had he been painted after the Synod of Whitby, in 664, he would have had a Roman one. Of course, the Book of Durrow could have been produced before 664 when Lindisfarne was a Celtic monastery, but prior to 664 Lindisfarne was a very modest institution, as Bede was at pains to say in his Ecclesiastical History.

In contrast, evidence to support the view that the Book of Durrow was made on Iona is available. Anglo-Saxon influence existed on Iona in the seventh century: King Oswald of Northumbria who ruled from c. 637–641 was on Iona himself for a while, and both Bede and Adomnan mention Oswald's overlordship over both the Picts and the

Figure 129 (opposite) A warrior with a Pictish type of shield is shown at the bottom of this page from the Book of Kells, late eighth century. (Photo: Trinity College Library, Dublin, MS 58, f. 200r)

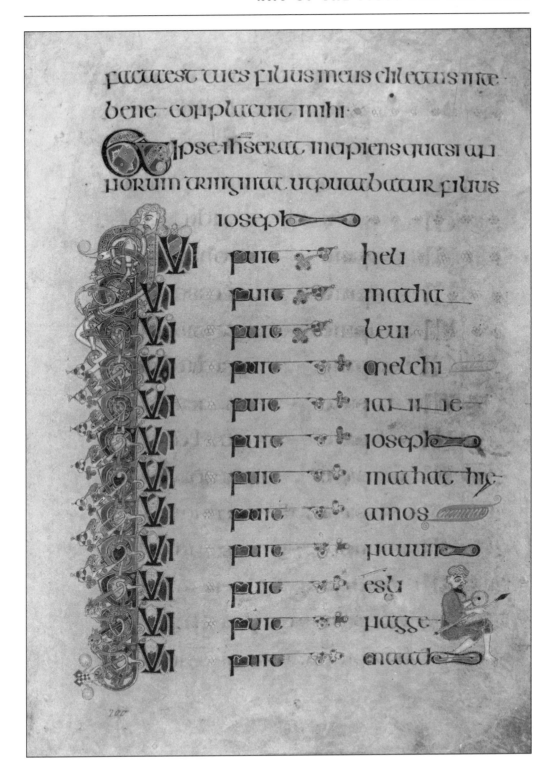

facuuest tues filius meus dilectus me
bene complacuit mihi
Ipse ihserat incipiens quasi an
horum triginta. ut putabatur filius
ioseph

VI	puit	heli
VI	puit	mattha
VI	puit	leui
VI	puit	melchi
VI	puit	iamne
VI	puit	ioseph
VI	puit	matthat hie
VI	puit	amos
VI	puit	hauum
VI	puit	esli
VI	puit	nagge
VI	puit	enaath

200

Figure 130 The Franks casket, a Northumbrian whalebone box with stylistic affinities to Pictish sculpture. This dates from around 700. Note particularly the Pictish-style animals at the bottom centre, and the figures similar to those on the Aberlemno chirchyard stone. It may have been carved by someone trained in a Pictish workshop. Length: 23.2 cm. (Photo: Trustees of the British Museum)

Scots. It is also known that there was a flourishing library on Iona. This possessed works on oriental hagiography and biblical exegesis. Adomnan referred to the library obliquely when he commented that, in his book on The Holy Places, he used excerpts from various writers that were available to him. The use of the Virgin Mary in Iona iconography may well be explained by oriental manuscripts in Iona (which may also account for the same iconography in the Book of Kells, later). It is also clear from archaeology that Anglo-Saxon objects were reaching Dunadd, and imported Mediterranean pottery was reaching Iona (see p. 51) in this period. Interlace similar to that in the Book of Durrow appears on an enamelled bronze mount from Dunadd. The arrangement of the evangelist symbols on the page with all four symbols is unusual, but accords with a Mediterranean model of Irenaeus, Bishop of Lyons. This model does not seem to have been available in Northumbria or in Ireland, but might again reflect Iona's library.

One last clue to the Book of Durrow's production on Iona is perhaps suggested by the fact that the scribe used defective sheets of vellum. This, it has been suggested, might point to a monastery that, because of its situation, had difficulty in obtaining new writing materials.

Dr George Henderson has argued that in the Book of Durrow, and in another manuscript which uses evangelist symbols without portraits, the Echternach Gospels, it is possible to see the inspiration of a lost Pictish manuscript, though there is no suggestion that the Echternach Gospels were actually produced in Pictland.

The Book of Kells is without doubt the finest of all the Insular manuscripts, and one of the greatest works of early medieval art. Now in Trinity College library in Dublin, it is usually regarded as an Irish product, illuminated at Kells in County Meath, or possibly begun on Iona and completed at Kells. In the arrangement of the text, the Book of Kells echoes that of the Book of Durrow. Either the Book of Kells copies the Book of Durrow, or they were both modelled on the same source. Dr Henderson has suggested that the source was at Iona, and that both books were taken to Ireland in 878, the Book of Kells having been produced on the occasion of the enshrining of St Columba, just as the Lindisfarne Gospels was probably produced on the occasion of the enshrining of St Cuthbert. If this is the case, the Book of Kells was perhaps produced in the mid- to late eighth century, perhaps between AD 752 and 767. The occasion for the transfer of the Book of Durrow and the Book of Kells, and along with them the shrine of St Columba, was undoubtedly the threat posed by Viking raids.

The Book of Kells is an intricate work, the product of several hands, and must have been extremely costly to produce. The funding may have come from royal as well as monastic patronage.

The Book of Kells uses full-page illustrations, and, in addition to Evangelist symbol pages and a carpet page it has the Temptation of Christ (the 'Temple Page'), the Betrayal, and the Virgin and Child, as well as portraits of Christ and the Evangelists. Particularly charming in the Book of Kells is the wealth of supporting detail – small figures of men and animals that serve as embellishments to the text pages.

The full complexity of the Book of Kells can best be appreciated from the 'Christi autem' page. The eye is stunned by the intricacy of the trumpet patterns, yin-yang scrolls, peltas and interlace. As one regards it, gradually the eye takes in the central subject – the monogram of Christ, Chi-Rho. As one continues to look the page, details in the ornament become apparent: here is an otter catching a fish, there are two cats with rats on their backs watching two rats eat a church wafer, next angels are noticed, and, at the centre, a scroll ending in a human head. This is not, however, mere whimsy on the part of the artist. Dr Henderson has argued very cogently that this is highly symbolic. The angels (and butterflies, which can also be detected) represent air, the cats earth and the otter, water. The whole he suggests is to be seen in terms of a text from Alcuin, alluding to the 'four rivers of the virtues flowing out of one bright and health-giving paradise'. The head on the end of the spiral is the head of Christ – the fountain of all energy.

The Pictish connotations of the Book of Kells are abundant and underline the strong influence of Pictish art on Iona. The Christi Autem page is closely paralleled in the ornament of the Nigg cross-slab, while the developed spiral patterns of the Book of Kells are shared by the Hilton of Cadboll slab and another at Shandwick in Easter Ross. The way in which key patterns are adapted to fit the available space is a feature of both the Book of Kells and Pictish slabs. In particular, similar key patterns can be found in the Book of Kells and in Pictish stones from Tarbat and Hilton of Cadboll. Many other devices are shared by the Book of Kells and Pictish sculptures, but do not seem to be generally

Figure 131 This page from the Book of Durrow (seventh century) depicts the evangelist symbol of a lion within an interlaced frame. It can be compared in its treatment with Pictish animals, for example the lion on the Papil stone (figure 97). (Photo: Trinity College Library, Dublin, MS 57, f. 191v)

widespread in Ireland or Northumbria. The naturalistic animals beloved of the artists of the Book of Kells are related to their counterparts in Pictland, and the occasional fantasy creature can also be found in both, for example the fish-tailed reptile that appears on stones at Murthly and Inchbrayock also appears on two folios in the Book of Kells. In figural work it has been pointed out that Pictish sculpture employs three styles, and the same three can be discerned in the Book of Kells. A human figure attacked by an animal is a recurrent theme in both. When all the details are compared and listed, as Dr Isabel Henderson has done, the catalogue is too long to be fortuitous. She has suggested that the reign of Oengus provides the context for the interchange of artistic elements. Oengus, the Pictish king, annexed Dalriada, and at various times allied himself with kings of Northumbria, Mercia and Wessex. It was suggested earlier (p. 155) that this reign was the most probable for the enshrinment of St Columba and, by extension, the creation of the Book of Kells. The patronage of Oengus could readily provide a context for the creation of a sumptuous and cosmopolitan work that the Book of Kells is known to be.

Iona, then, was one of the great centres of innovative sculpture and manuscript illumination. The evidence for metalwork is less clear, but the 'snake bosses' of the Iona crosses appear on two D-shaped objects now in St Germain Museum in France, which have been identified as the terminals of a very splendid house-shaped shrine. Two of the snakes have human heads, and resemble the head of Christ on the Christi Autem page in the Book of Kells. Where the St Germain terminals came from is unknown, but a similar pair, perhaps from the opposite end of the same shrine, has been found in a Viking woman's grave at Gausel in Norway. Could they have come from a shrine on Iona looted by the Vikings and, if so, could the shrine have been one produced at the time of the enshrining of St Columba?

Figure 132 These two chip-carved mounts from Crieff, Perthshire, probably came from a set of harness-mounts of a type fashionable in the later eighth/ninth century in Ireland (cf. Figure 35). A notable feature is the facing head which recalls those on the County Cavan brooch from Ireland. It has been suggested that it represents Christ (the bird heads also being seen as symbolic), but this is not very likely. Width: 4 cm. (Photo: Royal Museums of Scotland)

Although there is evidence for metalwork on Iona, the strongest evidence in Dalriada comes from Dunadd. Although no ornate bronzes were found at Dunadd, the moulds from the site show that a diversity of brooches, buckles and mounts were produced there. The brooches, in contrast to the fashion in Ireland, were true penannulars, and included versions with confronted hooked-beak bird heads on the terminals. These birds are echoed in the Book of Durrow eagle evangelist symbol and appear on the St Germain reliquary terminals.

A variant of the same bird heads appears decorating the terminals of the finest penannular brooch from Scotland, the Hunterston brooch. This brooch is in the same tradition as the famous Irish 'Tara' brooch in that it is not a true penannular but has both terminals joined together. It also follows Irish design in that the head of the pin, which is keystone-shaped, echoes the design of the terminals. The Hunterston brooch is decorated with amber studs and a wealth of gold filigree, including interlacing snakes and a pair of contorted animals attached to trays inset into the terminals. It also has crested bird heads which project from the hoop. Many of the features of the Hunterston brooch are closely related to Anglo-Saxon metalwork of the seventh century, and it has even been suggested that the brooch was made by an Anglo-Saxon craftsperson for a Celtic patron. The Hunterston brooch, most are agreed, is the earliest of the series of ornate brooches, and a date in the later seventh century is not impossible for it. It has a runic inscription on the back, added by a later Viking Age owner, who may well have looted it from Iona – although the inscription is in Scandinavian runes, his name was Irish (Melbrigda). The Anglo-Saxon connections of the brooch perhaps suggest it emanated from Dalriada. Although such brooches are usually regarded as secular, the original owner of the Hunterston brooch could have been the Church (the cross that appears between the terminals strengthens this suggestion), in which case Iona is again a likely provenance. The Hunterston brooch shares distinctive metalwork techniques with two other great pieces of Irish metalwork: the Derrynaflan paten and the Ardagh chalice. The technique, which both show, is also found on a brooch terminal (this time of a true penannular) found at Dunbeath, Caithness, which has a similar filigree animal on its terminal to that on the Hunterston brooch. The Dunbeath brooch is likely to be Pictish, perhaps pointing to an invention of the inlaid tray technique in Pictland and its adoption in Dalriada. If so, could the Derrynaflan paten and Ardagh chalice also have been produced on Iona? Mention has already been made of the similarity of the bird-nest bosses on the Iona crosses and the bosses on the Ardagh chalice. The latter also uses a type of angular lettering found in the Lindisfarne Gospels and in Pictland (on a stone from Tarbat, Inverness), which is believed to be Northumbrian and only represented in Ireland at Toureen Peakaun. Also, as already mentioned, the Derrynaflan paten has 'Anglo-Saxon' interlace best matched in the Book of Durrow. Many of the design elements on the Derrynaflan paten have their counterparts on Pictish stones.

Figure 133 The Breadalbane brooch. This silver brooch, named after Lord Breadalbane, is an Irish type of penannular brooch. It was modified in Pictland, where the terminals were sawn through and a Pictish pin added. It was drilled through and mounted in the nineteenth century. Diameter: 9.8 cm. (Photo: Trustees of the British Museum)

Figure 134 Bronze brooch from Mull. This is probably a Dalriadic product and a reminder that some penannulars were produced in Dalriada, as is shown by the moulds from Dunadd. (Photo Trustees of the British Museum)

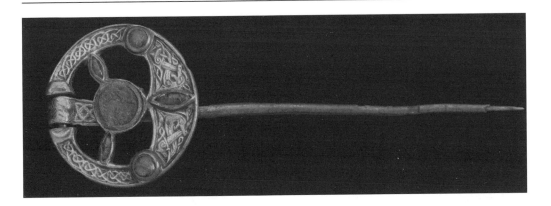

Figure 135 An Irish type of hinged pin from Dunipace, Stirling. This belongs to the same family as the more ornate Westness brooch. It could have been made in Ireland or Dalriada and is inlaid with amber/glass studs. Length: 11.3 cm. (Photo: Royal Museums of Scotland)

Wherever the Ardagh chalice and Derrynaflan paten were made, one ornate brooch again links Dalriada and Pictland. This is the Breadalbane brooch, named after the nineteenth-century collector, Lord Breadalbane. It was probably found in Perthshire, and was originally a pseudo–penannular which was imported into Pictland and 'modified' to suit Pictish taste – its terminals were sawn through and a Pictish type of replacement pin provided. The Breadalbane brooch could have been made in Ireland, and indeed the triple-cusped ornament on its terminals is most closely matched on a fine brooch from County Cavan, Ireland. The cusped pattern, however, is a distinctive feature of Pictish metalwork, and the panel of gold filigree on the hoop has a knot with a large-eyed snake which appears on Anglo-Saxon brooches.

A few other pieces of ornamental metalwork may have been made in Dalriada, but could have been imported there. For example, a plain penannular brooch with flaring terminals from Mull, which is an Irish type, or an ornate brooch of the later eighth century, also found on Mull. Like the Breadalbane brooch, the terminals of the latter were once joined but have been severed. However, the removal of the cross-bar in this case was probably not the work of Picts, but of nineteenth-century vandals.

Conclusion

The picture that emerges, then, of the art of the Picts and Scots is one of vigour, dynamism and brilliance, probably matching the comparable achievements of contemporary Ireland. Some of the artistic creations of the Picts and the Scots can be rated among the greatest art treasures of early medieval Europe: the Book of Durrow, the Book of Kells, the Nigg cross-slab, the St Andrews shrine, the Hunterston brooch and collectively the treasures of the St Ninian's Isle hoard. It was an artistic tradition in which there was constant interplay between the Picts and the Scots within northern Scotland, and it saw the profitable borrowing of ideas and motifs from Anglo-Saxon England, Ireland and the Continent.

Epilogue

What happened to the Picts and Scots after Kenneth mac Alpin amalgamated the two kingdoms in the ninth century? Clearly, the culture of Pictland did not disappear overnight, and the evidence from sculpture suggests that Pictish traditions lingered on to the end of the century, if not into the tenth. Some aspects of Pictish administration and land tenure seem to have persisted for some time, and it is likely that the Pictish language remained in use at least until the tenth century in some parts of Pictland. Some place-names seem to combine Pictish with Scots Gaelic elements. But, as has been seen, the two cultures of Picts and Scots were fundamentally very similar, and through a process of cross-fertilization had acquired traits, particularly artistic ones, from each other.

It is very likely that both cultures came closer together through the impact of a third – the Vikings. The Norse began their raiding on Scotland in the last years of the eighth century. Iona was first attacked in AD 795, and subsequently Norse settlement resulted in the colonization of the northern isles and north Scottish mainland, as well as many of the Hebridean islands.

In the northern isles, settlement began at the beginning of the ninth century, and it would seem from place-names and other sources that the Norse population was dominant. It has been estimated that 99 per cent of all Orkney place-names have Norse elements, and at least fifty thousand names in Shetland also appear to be Norse. A Norse earldom was esablished in Orkney around 880, and until the thirteenth century Orkney was the centre of a Scandinavian territory which extended to Shetland and Caithness. At first pagan, the earldom became Christian in the eleventh century, and the northern isles remained under Scandinavian domination until the fifteenth century.

It is therefore hardly surprising that Viking occupation succeeds Pictish on many sites in the northern isles. For example, Buckquoy in Orkney has Viking houses on top of Pictish, and a Viking burial and buildings succeed the Pictish phase at the Broch of Aikerness on Orkney, just as Viking structures swamped the Pictish on the Brough of Birsay. There is some evidence that the Vikings in Scotland may have borrowed some ideas from the Picts and Scots.

The Hebrides became linked to the Isle of Man in the Kingdom of Man and the Isles and, as many important Icelandic families came from the Hebrides, it is not surprising that the western isles are well documented in Icelandic sources. A saga relates how Ketill Flatnose became the first Norse ruler of the Hebrides in the ninth century. Archaeology bears this out, with the Hebrides producing a wealth of remains from the Viking Age. This includes a notable group of richly furnished ship burials, some of which contain Irish and Pictish objects.

The last mention of the Picts in Irish documentary sources appears in the early tenth century. Gradually, Scots Gaelic spread to become the dominant language throughout Scotland by the twelfth century. By this time, however, Norman influence had spread into Scotland. This process had begun in the time of Malcolm III, Canmore, who married a Saxon princess, St Margaret, and through her influence began the Anglicization of the Kingdom. It was furthered by David I who came to the throne in 1124. As the twelfth century advanced, the culture of most of Scotland fell into line with the rest of Britain. The Picts and Scots were no more.

Figure 136 Ornament on Pictish cross-slab, Shandwick, from Joseph Anderson, *Scotland in Early Christian Times* (1881)

Further Reading

General

The best, short introduction to the Picts, with beautiful colour illustrations, is A. Ritchie, *The Picts*, Edinburgh (1989), though it is written for the benefit of visitors to monuments in State care. The companion volume by D. Breeze and A. Ritchie, *Invaders of Scotland*, Edinburgh (1991), deals with the Scots, as well as with the Romans and Vikings, and is an equally good introduction. Short but useful, too, is I. Ralston and J. Inglis, *Foul Hordes: the Picts in the North-east and their Background*, Aberdeen (1984). This is primarily an exhibition catalogue, but has a very good introduction. Of the longer surveys, the classic remains F.T. Wainwright, *The Problem of the Picts*, Edinburgh (1955), which is particularly useful for art and history, as is I. Henderson, *The Picts*, London (1967). There is no book devoted to the Scots alone, though their history has been dealt with separately (see below). Two collections of papers are worth the attention of the serious student. These are J.G.P. Friell and W.G. Watson (eds), *Pictish Studies: Settlement, Burial and Art in Dark Age Northern Britain*, Oxford (1984); A. Small (ed), *The Picts: a New Look at Old Problems*, Dundee (1987). Although there are only a couple of key articles on the Picts in it, E. Meldrum (ed), *The Dark Ages in the Highlands*, Inverness (1971), is very useful. Three good studies can be found in K. Hughes, *Celtic Britain in the Early Middle Ages* (ed. D. Dumville), Woodbridge (1980). The Picts and Scots are set in a wider background in L. Laing, and J. Laing, *Celtic Britain and Ireland, c. AD 200–800*, Dublin (1990); L. Alcock, *Arthur's Britain*, London (1971); L. Laing, *The Archaeology of Late Celtic Britain and Ireland, c. 400–1200 AD*, London (1975). The Irish background to the Scots can be discovered in N. Edwards, *The Archaeology of Early Medieval Ireland*, London (1990).

History

The best historical introduction is A.P. Smyth, *Warlords and Holy Men*, London (1984). A short introduction can be found in A.A.M. Duncan, *Scotland: the Making of a Kingdom*, Edinburgh (1975). Somewhat learned for the general reader, but of fundamental importance, are

J. Bannerman, *Studies in the History of Dalriada*, Edinburgh (1974) (a collection of studies on the Scots); M.O. Anderson, *Kings and Kingship in Early Scotland*, Edinburgh (1973) (deals with both the Picts and the Scots). Of the older works, mention may be made of H.M. Chadwick, *Early Scotland*, Cambridge (1949); A.O. Anderson, *Early Sources of Scottish History, AD 500–1286*, 2 vols, Edinburgh (1922); and A.O. Anderson, and M. Anderson (eds), *Adomnan's Life of Columba*, Edinburgh (1961).

Prehistoric and Roman Scotland

The best summary is to be found in A. Ritchie and G. Ritchie, *Scotland*, 2nd Edn., London (1992), and the chapter (by I. Ralston) on the region in J.V.S. Megaw and D.D.A. Simpson, *Introduction to British Prehistory*, Leicester (1979). A recent collection of papers on the Iron Age can be found in I. Armit, (ed.), *Beyond the Brochs*, Edinburgh (1990). The Roman occupation of Scotland and the relationship of the Romans with the northern tribes can be found in D.J. Breeze, *Northern Frontiers of Roman Britain*, London (1982); W.S. Hanson and G.S. Maxwell, *Rome's North-west Frontier: the Antonine Wall*, Edinburgh (1988). Also very useful is G.S. Maxwell, *The Romans in Scotland*, Edinburgh (1989).

Some Key Sites

Excavations tend to be published in academic journals. Dundurn appears in L. Alcock, E. Alcock and S.T. Driscoll, 'Reconnaissance Excavations on Early Historic Fortifications and other Royal Sites in Scotland 3: Dundurn', in *Proceedings of the Society of Antiquaries of Scotland*, 119 (1989), 189–227, while Dunollie was reported by L. & E. Alcock, in *ibid.*, 117 (1987), 119–148. Clatchard Craig appears in J. Close-Brooks, 'Excavations at Clatchard Craig, Fife', in *ibid.*, 116 (1986), 117–84. No full report has appeared on the recent excavations at Dunadd, but J.H. Craw, 'Excavations at Dunadd and other Sites in the Poltalloch Estates, Argyll', in *ibid.*, LXIV (1929–30) is important. Iona is covered by the Royal Commission for Ancient and Historic Monuments of Scotland's *Argyll: an Inventory of the Monuments: IV, Iona*, Edinburgh, 1982.

Art

The best introductions are to be found in the general works listed above. In addition to these, however, might be mentioned S.H. Cruden (ed.), *The Early Christian Monuments of Scotland*, Edinburgh (1964); A. Jackson, *The Symbol Stones of Scotland*, Stromness, 1984; L.

Laing and J. Laing, 'The Date and Origin of the Pictish Symbols', in *Proceedings of the Society of Antiquaries of Scotland*, 114 (1984), 261–76; L. Laing and J. Laing, 'Archaeological Notes on some Scottish Early Christian Sculptures', in *ibid.*, 277–87; C. Curle, 'The Chronology of the Early Christian Monuments of Scotland', in *ibid.*, LXXIX (1939–40), 60–116; J.R. Allen and J. Anderson, *The Early Christian Monuments of Scotland*, Edinburgh (1903) (a classic work); A.C. Thomas, 'The Animal Art of the Scottish Iron Age and its Origins', in *Archaeological Journal*, CXVIII (1961), 14–64; A.C. Thomas, 'The Interpretation of the Pictish Symbols', in *ibid.*, CXX (1963), 31–97; A. Small, A.C. Thomas and D. Wilson, *St Ninian's Isle and its Treasure*, Aberdeen (1970) (the main publication on this famous hoard). The art of the Picts is set in perspective in L. Laing and J. Laing, *Art of the Celts*, London (1992). Manuscripts are discussed in G. Henderson, *From Durrow to Kells: The Insular Gospel Books 650–800*, London (1987).

Some readers may be interested to know of the Pictish Arts Society, which publishes a journal containing contributions from both professional and amateur students of Pictish art. Those interested in the society should write to the Membership Secretary, 17 Perth St, Edinburgh EH3.

Index

Numbers in *italic* type refer to figure numbers; those in **bold** type refer to colour plate numbers.